D1112119

PRESENTING

Paul
Zindel

TUSAS 540

Twayne's United States Authors Series
Young Adult Authors

General Editor: Patricia J. Campbell

The Young Adult Authors books seek to
meet the need for critical studies of fiction
for young adults. Each volume examines
the life and work of one author, helping
both teachers and readers of young adult
literature to understand better the writers
they have read with such pleasure
and fascination.

PRESENTING

Paul Zindel

Jack Jacob Forman

Twayne Publishers • Boston
A Division of G. K. Hall & Co.

Presenting Paul Zindel
Jack Jacob Forman

Copyright 1988 by G. K. Hall & Co.
All rights reserved.
Published by Twayne Publishers
A Division of G. K. Hall & Co.
70 Lincoln Street
Boston, Massachusetts 02111

Photographs and captions kindly provided by Paul Zindel

Copyediting supervised by Barbara Sutton
Book design by Barbara Anderson
Book production by Gabrielle B. McDonald
Typeset in 10/13 Century Schoolbook
by Modern Graphics, Inc., Weymouth, Massachusetts

Printed on permanent/durable acid-free paper
and bound in the United States of America

Library of Congress Cataloging–in–Publication Data

Forman, Jack Jacob.
    Presenting Paul Zindel / Jack Jacob Forman.
        p.   cm. — (Twayne's United States authors series ; TUSAS 540. Young
    adult authors)
    Bibliography: p.
    Includes index.
    ISBN 0–8057–8206–0 (alk. paper)
    1. Zindel, Paul—Criticism and interpretation.   2. Young adult fiction,
American—History and criticism.   I. Title.   II. Title: Paul
Zindel.   III. Series: Twayne's United States authors series ; TUSAS
540.   IV. Series: Twayne's United States authors series. Young adult
authors.
PS3576.I518Z68 1988
812'.54—dc19   88–513
                                                                                CIP

31144

To Meyer and Mish, Bill,
and the Tai Chi Queen

and for
Emily and Jennifer

Contents

PRESENTING PAUL ZINDEL

Preface

Almost twenty years ago, in my first professional librarian job, I had the good fortune to work for the progressive, service-oriented Free Public Library of Woodbridge, New Jersey. Although my experience in the field was limited, I had an abundance of wide-eyed enthusiasm and was hired to develop library programs for teenagers, or young adults, as the librarian and publisher professions call them.The library gave me free rein and much support in my work with this age group.

After having experienced surprising successes and all-out failures with the branch programs I had organized in my first three and a half years in the profession, I was assigned the job of trying to replicate some of the more successful programs at other library branches of this growing suburban township. With the invaluable help of the branch librarian, I set up a book discussion group with a small cluster of junior high–age readers. The first book I asked them to read was the novel *The Pigman* by Paul Zindel. None of the group had ever heard of it. When the book was published in hard cover three years before, it had won critical attention because it took its teenage characters seriously and on their own terms rather than casting them in adult stereotypes. In previous discussion groups I had led, I had selected only classics or contemporary adult novels, because until *The Pigman* was published I had not been able to find a young adult novel worth discussing.

It was a wonderful choice. It galvanized the young teens, and they talked and talked and talked about the book, long past the time I had planned to end the session. It encouraged me to try other recently published young adult novels with groups of teen readers, and I soon became aware that the publication of Zindel's story had been instrumental in clearing the way for a new generation of youth fiction.

So when Ron Brown of the Boston Public Library called me in San Diego twelve years later and invited me to write this book, I instinctively said yes. And I am glad I did, although I must have set a record for procrastination. Writing the book, I learned a great deal about why *The Pigman* had struck such a chord of response in teenagers and why Zindel's unique mixture of the macabre and the moral continues to fascinate and entertain young readers today.

For this opportunity, I thank Ron Brown whose thoughtful criticism and warm support kept me going at the early stages of my writing. I am also immensely grateful to Patty Campbell, the current editor of this series and author of its first title, a model of literary criticism and lively prose. Her excellent advice and on-target suggestions helped me focus and structure this book, and her patience and understanding encouraged me to finish my work. In addition, I thank Athenaide Dallett of Twayne Publishers for her willingness to redefine the word *deadline* and Cecile Watters for her expert copyediting and sound suggestions.

I owe a debt of gratitude to librarians Phil Smith and Elliot Kanter of the University of California, San Diego Central Library for invaluable research help and advice, to Shirley Bischoff of the Mesa College Library in San Diego for bibliographic verification, and to Alleen Pace Nilsen for background information. I thank Charlotte Zolotow, Paul Zindel's editor at Harper & Row, for taking the time to speak with me about his works, and I thank Bill Morris at Harper for supplying me with copies of Zindel's novels. Finally, Paul Zindel's open and honest interviews with me were invaluable sources of information. Without his cooperation and kindness, this book would not have been possible.

To all the above, I extend my thanks. But the one who deserves the most recognition is my wife, Gail, who—although impatient with my bad working habits—gave me support and advice that only she could give.

Jack Jacob Forman

Mesa Community College

Chronology

1936   Paul Zindel born 15 May in Staten Island, New York.

1951–1952   Contracts tuberculosis; enters sanitorium during junior year of high school. Returns to school eighteen months later.

1954   Graduates from Port Richmond High School on Staten Island.

1954–1958   Attends Wagner College and receives a B.S. in chemistry.

1957   Father dies.

1958   Hired as technical writer for Allied Chemical Co.

1959   Awarded M.S. in education at Wagner College. *Dimensions of Peacocks,* his first play, produced.

1959–1969   Teaches chemistry and physics at Tottenville High School on Staten Island.

1960   *Euthanasia and the Endless Hearts,* his second play, produced.

1962   *A Dream of Swallows* produced.

1965   *The Effect of Gamma Rays on Man-in-the-Moon Marigolds* first produced in Houston's Alley Theatre.

1966–1967   Takes sabbatical from teaching and becomes playwright-in-residence at Houston's Alley Theatre. National Education Television (NET) productions of *Let Me Hear You Whisper* (a play) and a shortened version of *Gamma Rays.*

1968 *The Pigman,* his first novel, published. Mother dies.

1969 *My Darling, My Hamburger* published.

1970 *I Never Loved Your Mind* published. Plays *Let Me Hear You Whisper* and *The Effect of Gamma Rays on Man-in-the-Moon Marigolds* published. *Gamma Rays* first produced in New York. Wins Obie Award.

1971 The play *And Miss Reardon Drinks A Little* published and first produced. *Gamma Rays* republished and awarded Pulitzer Prize and other honors. Awarded honorary doctorate of humanities by Wagner College. Writes screenplay *Mrs. Beneker* (never produced).

1972 The play *The Secret Affairs of Mildred Wild* first produced in New York. Screenplay *Up the Sandbox* produced by NET and First Artists Films.

1973 Marries Bonnie Hildebrand, 25 October. Plays *The Ladies Should Be in Bed* and *The Secret Affairs of Mildred Wild* published. Twentieth Century–Fox film production of *Gamma Rays* produced by Paul Newman, starring Joanne Woodward.

1974 *Let Me Hear You Whisper* republished. Son, David, born.

1975 *I Love My Mother,* children's picture book, published. Screenplay *Mame* produced by Warner Brothers. Play *Ladies at the Alamo* first produced.

1976 *Pardon Me, You're Stepping on My Eyeball* published. Daughter, Lizabeth, born.

1977 *Confessions of a Teenage Baboon* published. *Ladies at the Alamo,* a play, published.

1978 *The Undertaker's Gone Bananas* published.

1980 *The Pigman's Legacy* published. *A Star for the Latecomer,* a novel co-authored with Bonnie Zindel, published.

Chronology

1981 *The Girl Who Wanted a Boy* published.

1982 *To Take a Dare,* a novel co-authored with Crescent Dragonwagon, published.

1984 *Harry and Hortense at Hormone High* published. Screenplay *Maria's Lovers* produced by Cannon Films. *When a Darkness Falls,* adult novel, published.

1985 Screenplay of *Runaway Train* produced by Cannon Films. *Alice in Wonderland and Through the Looking-Glass,* musical TV special, produced.

1986 *Babes in Toyland,* musical TV special, produced.

1987 *The Amazing and Death-Defying Diary of Eugene Dingman* published.

1. Conflicts and Lessons: The Life of Paul Zindel

In Paul Zindel's latest young adult novel, *The Amazing and Death-Defying Diary of Eugene Dingman,* the winningly innocent fifteen-year-old narrator records in his diary some recent events in his life: "Two months ago, my mother, Mrs. Brenda Dingman, rented our cellar to a man called Charlie Mayo who walks with a limp and wheezes like a godfather. Right after that, my mother started wearing a lot of makeup for the first time since almost six years ago when my father moved out of our lower-middle-class split-level and went to live with a statuesque secretary."[1] A couple of paragraphs later, Eugene reveals that his older sister, Penelope, hates their policeman father for his failure to support them as he had promised. Soon afterward, Eugene also writes that his Aunt Ruth has gotten him a summer job as a waiter at the Lake Henry Hotel in the Adirondacks.

The names, for the most part, have been changed, but in these first three pages of Paul Zindel's tenth young adult novel, readers are introduced to a slice of the author's life and a representative sample of his family:

- His single-parent mother who became romantically involved with a boarder when Zindel was fifteen.
- His policeman father who left Zindel's mother to live with another woman.

- His older sister who hated his father for abandoning the family.
- His aunt, Matilda Rowan, his father's sister, who helped the author, his mother, and his sister after his father left.
- Charlie Mayo, the real name of the boarder whom Zindel's mother dated. They used to leave the house separately, go in opposite directions, double back, and meet each other behind the house—and then go out on a date.[2]
- Zindel's first job—a waiter at the Sagamore Hotel on Lake George in the Adirondacks. He worked summers there from the time he was sixteen until he reached twenty-one.

"I write only about the things I know," Zindel told an audience of school librarians nine years ago.[3] The year before, in a published interview, he said, "As a writer, I am a historian and write from life models."[4] In a recent interview, Zindel modified "life models" to "living images" to indicate that his characters are not simply replicas but a composite of others and himself.[5] Not all of Zindel's young adult novels contain characters and situations as closely drawn from the author's life as those that appear in his latest novel. Nevertheless, to understand the "living images" and themes of his stories for teenagers, the reader should know Zindel's personal history because it so infuses his books.

Paul Zindel was born on Staten Island in 1936. His father, Paul, was a policeman who, when Zindel was two years old, deserted his family to live with a woman he had met on his beat. As Zindel recounts it, his father was making his daily rounds and walked into a bar, passing a woman sitting on a bar stool. "Officer," she said, "you wouldn't give a lady a ticket for parking on a stool too long, would you?" This remark began a satisfying and happy relationship that lasted until his father's death in 1957. Zindel holds no hard feelings against the woman—the author's two children today even call her Grandma. But he does resent his father; not only did the elder Zindel break up the family and fail to support them, but he neglected his son. With deep regret, Zindel says that he saw his father no more than ten times after he left the family. "There was no room for me in his life," he reflects sadly.[6]

Zindel's mother, Beatrice Mary Frank Zindel, was left to raise him and his sister, Betty, who was two years older. Brought up by Irish Catholic parents, Beatrice had stopped practicing Catholicism soon after her marriage to Zindel's father, whose ancestry was German Lutheran. One day, she heard shouting in front of her house, looked out, and saw a priest parading up and down the sidewalk screaming over and over again, "You're not married in the Catholic Church!" The embarrassment of this experience, however, was far surpassed by her subsequent shock when she discovered that her husband had contracted syphilis. Although he was treated successfully, Zindel believes his mother never forgave his father, and he thinks this was a precipitating factor in their breakup.[7]

In the years following their separation, Beatrice Zindel worked in a variety of jobs and dragged her son and daughter to new living quarters almost every year. Zindel recalls that during World War II, his mother worked as a shipyard riveter and later as a hatcheck girl, a waitress, a breeder of collie dogs, and a food concessionaire at an airport and at nightclubs. But her primary job was practical nursing. She often took assignments that required a family move from one place to another on Staten Island and that involved short-term around-the-clock nursing care for terminally ill patients.[8]

Zindel thinks his mother was always insecure because of her lack of formal education and her poor immigrant family background. This social uncertainty, however, was greatly magnified after her marital break, and she became paranoid and developed sexual neuroses. She also feared death and had a recurring nightmare about a rat leaping at her in the cellar, until, at the last moment, a cat would kill the rodent. Despite her emotional instability, however, Beatrice Zindel befriended many who called on her for advice, especially those "in a lower station of life." Because they were not a social threat, she was generous and giving of her time.[9]

When Zindel's mother died of cancer in 1968, the author was

devastated. She had died in an excruciatingly painful way, and he was powerless to help her. He also felt guilty because he had always wanted to do something to make her difficult life better. Soon after he won the Pulitzer Prize in 1971, he dreamed that he offered his mother money to go on a world tour. But she said—in his dream—that "she wasn't able to go because she was dead."[10]

Despite his guilt about his mother, Zindel believes that her low self-esteem and social insecurity were legacies "handed to him on a platter."[11] "I never liked myself physically," he says today. Looking good to feel good was not part of his growing-up experience, partly because of his mother's financial problems and partly because of her negative attitudes. He aimed for a bland, neutral look. "My clothing style was called insignificant. If I could achieve that, I was happy," he recalls.[12]

Zindel's childhood was rootless and lonely. The constant moving and his mother's periods of depression took their toll. "There were no peers; there were no friends. There was no one to talk to," he remembers.[13] Even his hobbies were solitary: homemade marionettes, aquariums, insectariums, and terrariums.[14] The isolation he felt as a result of his childhood insecurities was further intensified by a one-and-a-half-year struggle with tuberculosis when he was fifteen. He had the misfortune to fall sick just before drugs were developed to treat the disease. Although he had a "minimal case" of the illness, he was sent to a sanatorium in upstate New York and spent eighteen months of his formative years in a world of very sick adults. Had he been able to be treated with drugs, he estimates he would have been cured in two months.[15]

Those eighteen months interrupted his high school education, but when he recovered Zindel was determined to get his life back on track. In grade school, he had appeared in a couple of plays and earlier in high school he had adapted or written short plays and skits (including one based on W. W. Jacob's famous short story, "The Monkey's Paw").[16] Upon returning to school, he entered a playwriting contest sponsored by the American Cancer Society and won a silver ballpoint pen for his first full-length play—an upbeat drama about a very sick pianist who recovers to play Chopin's *Warsaw* Concerto at Carnegie Hall (he had been introduced to this piece of music at the sanatorium).[17]

In his senior year at Port Richmond High School, everything came to a head—his unsatisfying family life, his resentment over his stay in the sanitorium, and what Zindel calls general "teenage angst." One day, he lowered his suitcase down a clothesline from his upper-story apartment and ran off to Miami, Florida. Staying at the YMCA, he tried unsuccessfully to get a job at the *Miami News.* But after two weeks of futile efforts, he exhausted his limited financial resources and ended his adventure as abruptly as he had begun it.[18]

Not knowing what he wanted to do or where he wanted to go, Zindel graduated from high school a year late and applied to five colleges. Although he was accepted at prestigious schools like Colgate and Cornell, he decided to commute to Wagner College on Staten Island because he had "no money and no vision." He remembers being disappointed with his decision because Wagner lacked the advanced scientific equipment available at the larger universities.[19]

Zindel majored in chemistry at Wagner, but after editing the school paper and contributing to its literary magazine, he tried to change to literature and drama in his junior year. The school, however, discouraged this move because of the promising job prospects for chemistry graduates; counselors at the school even threatened to take away his scholarship funds if he switched majors. He decided to stay with chemistry, but he renewed his interest in theater when he took a course in Continental drama and submitted an original play as his term paper.[20]

Two other events during these last two years in college reinforced Zindel's interest in drama. As editor of the school newspaper, he assigned himself to cover a New York writers' conference at which playwright Edward Albee was scheduled to speak. Zindel was so enthralled by Albee's talk that he ended up taking a course taught by him. Under the famous playwright's direction, Zindel wrote a play called *Dimensions of Peacocks,* which not coincidentally was about a disturbed teenager whose domineering mother is a visiting nurse who steals petty items from her patients. (The play is a forerunner of *Confessions of a Teenage Baboon.*)[21]

During a summer recess when Zindel worked as a waiter in the Adirondacks, he met a young actor named John Foster who was involved in New York City's theatrical scene. Foster introduced him to the first professional dramatic productions Zindel had ever seen—Lillian Hellman's *Toys in the Attic,* with Maureen Stapleton, productions of absurdists like Eugène Ionesco, and those of the European avant-garde such as Kurt Weill.[22]

When he graduated from Wagner College with a degree in chemistry in 1958, Zindel was torn between the need for a job that would use his scientific education and the attraction of his real interest—writing. He decided to combine the two: he accepted a job at Allied Chemical as a technical writer. But within six months he had become bored with the work and the nine-to-five routine and was unhappy about his long commute on the Staten Island ferry. "The day I quit," Zindel remembers, "I was so happy, I cried."[23]

He looked around for other jobs to which he could apply his training and decided to give high school teaching a chance. Returning to Wagner College, he completed a master's program in education the following year and was hired as a physics and chemistry teacher at Tottenville High School on Staten Island. Zindel says that his first two years there were very difficult because he was afraid of teaching and was too much in need of approval from his students and colleagues to be effective. In 1963, however, the situation improved when a new principal arrived and began after-school in-service training sessions for his faculty. This gave Zindel the confidence he needed and enabled him to concentrate on teaching rather than worrying about status and competency.[24]

But his interest in theater was never far from his mind, and he spent his summers writing plays. He had begun to realize that doing five lesson plans a day was "really like structuring five one-act plays."[25] After two minor plays failed to attract critical attention or public approval (*Euthanasia and the Endless Hearts* and *A Dream of Swallows*), in the summer of 1963 he wrote *The Effect of Gamma Rays on Man-in-the-Moon Marigolds,* which borrowed liberally from his collection of living images. The following year it was accepted for production in Houston's Alley Theatre.

Zindel's increasing absorption in drama was beginning to detract from his commitment to teaching. In 1966, he took a leave of absence from his high school position to accept a Ford Foundation playwright-in-residence award at the Alley Theatre, where he learned more about the production aspects of drama. When he returned to teaching twelve months later, he noticed a marked change in his students. They seemed less interested in learning, and many, he noticed, were so stoned on drugs that they were not even aware they were in school. "I was teaching academic chemistry, and they were off somewhere in another world," Zindel recalls.[26] Disillusioned and unable to relate to these social changes, he concluded that "what I was teaching no longer had any purpose. I had no goal, and I felt stupid going to work."[27] So Zindel quit to spend more time writing plays and developing his skill in a new occupation—writing novels for teenagers.

A year before, Charlotte Zolotow, a children's book editor at the publishing house of Harper & Row, had chanced to watch a television adaptation of *Gamma Rays* because her friend Eileen Heckart played a leading role in the production. (Barbara Dana, another actress in that same adaptation, is now an author under Zolotow's editorial direction.)[28] Zolotow was greatly moved by the play, especially by the pain and anguish of the alcoholic mother. But it was her enthusiasm for Zindel's characterizations of teenagers and his flare for writing realistic, colorful dialogue that prompted her to call the playwright. She arranged a meeting to discuss the possibility of his writing a young adult novel—a story for and about teenagers. Zolotow persuaded Zindel that his writing skills and his understanding of adolescents were especially suited for the genre. Before accepting her proposal, however, he investigated what had been written for this age group. "I researched the form and drew upon my years of teaching high school," he says.[29] What he discovered about the past failures and the future promise of this neglected form of literature made him want to try his hand at it.

Given his recent disenchantment with teaching and the memory of his own tempestuous adolescence, it is not surprising that his first drafts produced some very dark and extreme characters, all of them much alike. Zolotow encouraged him to downplay some of the parental caricatures he had created and provide more of a distinction between his protagonists and antagonists. She also helped direct the new author toward creating more clearly individuated characters.[30]

The Pigman was the result of his first efforts, and it met with immediate critical acclaim—and even more important, enthusiastic acceptance from teenagers. Its success and that of *My Darling, My Hamburger* two years later helped Zindel justify the decision to end his teaching career and devote all his time to writing.

In 1970, six years after it was first produced in Houston, *Gamma Rays* finally reached the New York City stage. It initially appeared off Broadway, but when a fire destroyed the theater, it was moved to Broadway where it ran for 819 performances. Orin Lehman, the play's producer, had submitted *Gamma Rays* as a candidate for the 1971 Pulitzer Prize without Zindel's knowledge, so it came as a complete surprise when he learned that he had won. At the time, Zindel was living on Staten Island. He remembers that he was watching the movie *King Kong* at a friend's apartment in Manhattan when another friend burst through the door shouting, "Oh, God, it's incredible!" "What's going on?" Zindel responded. "Didn't you hear?" his friend said. "You won the Pulitzer Prize!" Stunned, Zindel called his answering service and found that the national press had been trying to contact him. On his trip back to Staten Island, he got a ticket for speeding, but he was only half aware of what was happening.[31]

The prize, as it turned out, was only a thousand dollars, but Zindel soon found that there were considerable residual benefits associated with the honor. It gave him national recognition, which led to a film adaptation of *Gamma Rays* produced and directed by Paul Newman and starring Joanne Woodward. Following this, he was offered several screenplay opportunities. He immediately set to work learning this new skill, and in rapid succession, he wrote three screenplays: *Mrs. Beneker,* an unproduced work based on Violet Weingarten's popular novel; *Up the Sandbox,* based on a story by Anne Roiphe; and *Mame,* adapted from Patrick Dennis's best-seller, *Auntie Mame.*

The Pulitzer Prize also promoted the Broadway productions of *Gamma Rays* and a new play entitled *And Miss Reardon Drinks a Little.* This quick rise to fame, however, extracted a price. The combination of fast money, instant success, and quick stardom induced great stress. While on a vacation in Mexico, he had an attack of tachycardia which made him feel that "his heart was jumping out of his chest." Although he hesitated to seek medical attention in Mexico because of the language barrier and because he was dubious about the quality of the medical care, he was more afraid of dying. So he rushed to a doctor—who told him in broken English, "You are going to die." Zindel's first reaction was panic, but then some part of his brain told him to question the doctor further. "You mean I am going to die?" Zindel asked. "I am going to die? I will definitely die? I shall die? I could have died?" "Yeah," the doctor said, correcting his tenses. "You could have died."[32]

Although Zindel recovered from this scare and the tachycardia, he suffered a breakdown from nervous exhaustion. Returning to New York City, he entered psychoanalysis. What helped most, however, in putting his life together during these hectic years was his involvement with Bonnie Hildebrand. Six months before *Gamma Rays* opened in New York, Zindel had gone to the Cleveland Playhouse where the play was being staged. At the time, Bonnie was the publicity director and was unhappily married for the second time to the same man, a psychologist. Like Zindel, she had—a few years before—lost her mother to cancer and was very interested in the theater and writing.

"Lovely, bubbly, and very outgoing" were his first impressions of her, but their courtship was not a quick one.[33] It took Bonnie (who was seven years younger than Zindel) many months more to realize that she did not want to continue living with her husband. When she finally separated from him and came to New York to live with Zindel, he in turn resisted becoming seriously involved because he did not want anyone telling him what to do around the house. But as he spent some time away from Bonnie, he came to realize how much he loved her. In 1973, while traveling alone in Europe—four years after they had met—he called her and proposed. They were married on 25 October 1973 in Westminster, England, in a civil ceremony that began bizarrely. Zindel had rented a 1936 Rolls-Royce to carry them to the ceremony. When they arrived, however, guards whisked his wife-to-be out of the car to another wedding, thinking she was the bride in *that* ceremony. These same attendants then asked Zindel if he was the father of the bride![34]

The Zindels moved back to New York to live. In the next six years, they had two children—David, born in 1974, and Lizabeth, born two years later. During this time, Zindel wrote three young adult novels—*Pardon Me, You're Stepping on My Eyeball, Confessions of a Teenage Baboon,* and *The Undertaker's Gone Bananas*—probably the three most cathartic and confessional of his novels for teenagers.

As his family grew, Zindel looked for opportunities to earn more money to support his wife and children, and he found a lucrative prospect in Hollywood, writing screenplays. He was also attracted by the more open space there. Manhattan was too crowded for his taste, and he missed the spacious greenery he remembered from his childhood on Staten Island. So in 1978 he moved his family to Beverly Hills. But he soon found that the life-style he was expected to follow required more and more money, and he felt himself caught in an upward-spiraling cycle. He lost sight of artistic objectives, and money became his goal. "I had my priorities mixed up," he admits. "Money should always serve to support one's talents. Talents can never be used to support the money."[35]

During the early eighties, Zindel published two more young adult novels—*The Pigman's Legacy* and *The Girl Who Wanted a Boy.* Although critics differed on their merits, Zindel himself says that he invested little of himself in the books; he wrote them mainly for money. Also written for money and fame was his only adult novel, a sordid and sensationalized suspense story entitled *When a Darkness Falls.* It was set in Los Angeles with characters analogous to his family, and its preoccupation with neurotic and

Paul's father, Paul Eugene Zindel.

At age one with four-year-old sister, Betty.

At age six with Betty.

Paul *(left)* at age ten with cousin
Jack and a friend.

At age twelve at a dude ranch.

At fifteen with fellow patients at Stony Wold Tuberculosis
Sanatorium, Lake Kushagua, New York.

Paul *(center)* on the night of his junior prom.

At eighteen, off duty from his job as a waiter at the Sagamore Hotel, Lake George, New York.

With Betty *(left)* and mother, Beatrice. at his graduation from Wagner College in 1958.

The playwright holds Janus masks, 1975.

With wife, Bonnie, and children Lizabeth and David.

With Lizabeth and David, rowing on the Serpentine, London, 1978.

With Shelly Winters on the set of *The Effect of Gamma Rays on Man-in-the-Moon Marigolds,* Long Beach, California during 1977–78 season before the production moved to New York.

Paul Zindel, 1982.

At the Marilyn Monroe Theatre, located in Los Angeles and part
of the Lee Strasberg Institute, 1982.

With actress Drew Barrymore on the set of the NBC production of
Babes in Toyland, Munich, West Germany, 1986.

psychotic behavior mirrored Zindel's feeling that his artistic life was out of control.

It was during these same years that he attached his name to two young adult novels he helped others write: *A Star for the Latecomer,* written by his wife, and *To Take a Dare,* written by Crescent Dragonwagon (Charlotte Zolotow's daughter). His main contribution to both was advice on structure and focus.

In fact, many of his Hollywood screenplays were also written in collaboration with others. For Zindel, it was a period of straying from his "moral and artistic focus," and when he realized what was happening to him, he and Bonnie moved the family back to New York in 1985.[36] Zindel looks upon this not as a rejection of Hollywood—he still writes screenplays that require frequent trips to the West Coast—but as a reaffirmation of his desire to work alone toward his literary goals and to refuse projects for which he feels no empathy. "I have got to be strongly connected to what I am doing next," Zindel says. "I don't want to do any more books which are written without strong emotional feelings." Such emotion is central to Zindel's measure of a good book: "If I cry at the end of the novel, then I know there is some element of worth to it for me."[37]

In the last three years, Zindel has published two widely varying young adult novels: *Harry and Hortense at Hormone High* and *The Amazing and Death-Defying Diary of Eugene Dingman.* The former concerns the mythic roots of our society and the values of contemporary Western civilization; the latter deals more directly with Zindel's own life. Both indicate that the author is once again back on track, writing about "only the things I know." Zindel says that for the first time since he wrote *The Undertaker's Gone Bananas* he cried after writing the climactic scenes to each of his two most recent novels.

What Paul Zindel knows best is drawn from his life—his family, his experiences, his values. He has explored themes important to him: self-identity, responsibility, adult authority, sexual roles, and death. Certain patterns of thought about each of these subjects can be discerned, and these patterns can be traced to Zindel's reflections on his life and the living images he has constructed.

2. Conflicts and Lessons: The Young Adult Novels of Paul Zindel

When Charlotte Zolotow twenty years ago suggested to Paul Zindel that he try his hand at writing novels for teenagers, she was speaking to someone whose creative writing interests and experience were until then limited to drama for adult audiences. In fact, it was a television adaptation of *Gamma Rays* before its New York production that convinced the editor Zindel had a special understanding of and feeling for teenage characters. Even today, Zindel asserts that his major talent is placing actors in a set and putting them in conflict.[1] (He also admits that, after his survey of the field in 1967, he has not read any more young adult novels.)[2]

Since *The Pigman*, Zindel has tried a variety of literary forms, including plays, screenplays, teleplays, a picture book for preschool children, and a sexually explicit novel for adults. But aside from his Pulitzer Prize–winning play, his reputation rests on his popular stories for teenagers—a body of works that includes ten novels and two others he has co-authored. His success as a young adult novelist can be attributed to the mix of his thespian skills with his basic thematic ideas and structural guidelines, all permeated with the raw material of his own life.

In all his young adult novels, Zindel tries to create "a protagonist and an antagonist plus a third person who's involved in the climax." Often this translates into a teen hero, an adult foil, and another teenager of the opposite sex who helps the protagonist "through a series of adventures and conflicts and challenges." The hero, however, is not a superman of virtue; he (it is usually a male) is a person with many problems who is changed by his encounters and who "lifts the reader's insights."[3]

Zindel's characters are created from an amalgam of his life— a composite of people the author has known whom he calls "living images."[4] Usually, he begins the creative process of character formation by focusing on one person he has known. He labels this acquaintance an "inspirational homunculus."[5] (A "homunculus," according to a medieval theory, was a "fully-formed miniature human body" thought to be part of the human sperm.)[6] As Zindel's fictional character begins to take shape from a blend of these living images, the author projects himself onto the new being he has created. "I lay on [the character] my own childhood and my teenage years," Zindel says.[7] "You end up writing about yourself, but you don't know it."[8]

The author uses the fully formed creations to inspire themselves, his readers, and most of all himself. "All my characters learn a lesson," Zindel told an interviewer a decade ago.[9] More recently, he has said that "all artistic expression is a result of a compulsion to solve problems."[10] He readily admits that his writing for young adults is the result of an "interrupted adolescence" and that his stories "solve his own problems" left unresolved from those years.[11] His novels, therefore, lift his own insight as well as his readers'.

Zindel's young adult novels also consistently adhere to a set of guidelines that form a decalogue of writing in the genre:

1. Stories should relate in part to school environments since this is where teenagers spend most of their time.
2. Parents should be in the background because teenagers are interested in putting distance between themselves and their guardians.
3. Stories should be told by the teenage characters—or at least from their viewpoint.

4. The language and dialogue should be contemporary, but not trendy.
5. Romance and the characters' awkward attempts at it should be incorporated into the stories.
6. Pretense and phoniness should be avoided.
7. Teenagers like mischief and rebellion in novels because they resent being ruled by adult society.
8. Fast-paced action and suspense are essential.
9. "Transitional pictures" such as graffiti, letters, and doodling break up the linear print and simulate how teens often communicate.
10. Stories should be short.[12]

Underpinning these guidelines is a commitment to write realistically about the concerns of teenagers. It is this commitment, according to Kenneth Donelson and Alleen Pace Nilsen, that distinguished the early young adult novels of Zindel—and those of authors such as S. E. Hinton, Robert Cormier, and John Donovan—from the previous genre of teen fiction calcified in the gender and age stereotypes of the 1950s. Donelson and Nilsen, in their authoritative survey, *Literature for Today's Young Adults,* note that in the late 1960s Zindel's first book, *The Pigman,* was a ground-breaking novel because it turned away from past pieties and established a new type of adolescent fiction in which teenagers dealing with interpersonal or societal problems were depicted with candor and seriousness.[13]

One has only to look over the American Library Association's Best Books for Young Adults lists from the 1960s to realize what was ground-breaking about Zindel's first novel. Unlike recent lists, the compilations of the sixties consisted of largely *adult* fiction and nonfiction considered to be relevant, accessible, and worthwhile for teenage readers. Why the Best Books committees ignored or passed over the very books published for this age group is a complex issue. But surely one reason relates to the fact that fiction written at that time for young people was pedestrian, predictable, and formulaic—meant to satisfy adult stereotypes of adolescence. What was revolutionary about *The Pigman* and *The*

Outsiders was that they portrayed teenagers living their lives uncolored by adult preconceptions. In fact, both novels failed to make the Best Books list in the years they were published, although both were voted onto a composite list called Best of the Best Books for Young Adults, compiled in 1975. Both books, however, did help change the direction of these lists; by the early 1970s, the annual selections contained works by both Zindel and Hinton, as well as other writers who followed their lead.

The Pigman is still the book against which most of Zindel's critics measure his later works. In alternate first-person narrative chapters, John Conlan and Lorraine Jensen—teenagers alienated from crazy parents, an irrelevant school, and insensitive classmates—tell a story that changes their lives.[14]

"Now, I don't like school," John begins the book's first chapter—and immediately the reader is pulled into the story. Four pages later, the reader learns that the man known as the Pigman has died suddenly and tragically and that the two teenage narrators have played some role in his death. As John and Lorraine relate what happened, they talk about the mischievous pranks and practical jokes they and their friends often relish. One of these games consists of calling people at random and trying to keep them on the phone as long as possible. Posing as a charity representative, John succeeds so well with a Mr. Pignati that he gets himself and Lorraine invited to visit the next afternoon.

The two teenagers find a lonely old man who accepts them as friends and teaches them challenging games. They call him the Pigman because of his large and treasured collection of glass, clay, and marble pigs. Mr. Pignati tells John and Lorraine that his wife is in California, but to their shock, they uncover evidence in the old man's attic that she is dead. As each day passes, the two alienated teenagers grow closer to this solitary man who cannot face up to the reality of his wife's death. To reciprocate their friendship, Mr. Pignati takes John and Lorraine to the zoo and introduces them to a baboon named Bobo to whom the old man has become attached. Later, while playing a roller-skating game at home, the Pigman suffers a near-fatal heart attack. As he recuperates in the hospital, John impulsively decides to have a party in Mr. Pignati's empty house. This, however, soon turns into a riot: the collection of pigs is smashed, and the house is devastated. Just at this point, Mr. Pignati arrives home from the hospital.

A few days later, a remorseful John and Lorraine meet their now broken and demoralized friend at the zoo, and they discover that Bobo died the day before. Upon hearing this news, the Pigman suffers a massive and fatal heart attack. The two teenagers are left to ponder their complicity in his death and to face accepting responsibility for their actions in this tragedy.

Each of the three main characters in Zindel's novel was a life image drawn from someone Zindel had known. John was a sixteen-year-old boy the author reprimanded for trespassing on the grounds of a Staten Island castle where Zindel was house-sitting one summer. Although the boy was initially "angry and explosive" when Zindel confronted him, the two soon became friends. The author learned that John was on probation as a result of fighting at a block party. Zindel connected the boy's anguish and rebelliousness to his own "floating anguish" when he ran away to Miami. Lorraine was based on "a lonely, teary-eyed girl" in one of his classes— a girl who was "always thinking about death or war." Onto her character, Zindel layered his own feelings of vulnerability and inferiority.[15]

The Pigman was a complex composite. At the top of the castle where Zindel first met John was a Byzantine tower that required a ladder to reach it. One day, Zindel was in the tower when an old man yelled at him from the ground, saying that he wanted to buy an old DeSoto that Zindel had advertised for sale. Climbing down, he followed the eccentric back to his house where the car changed hands for two hundred dollars. The old man's sister confided to Zindel that her brother's wife had died and that he could not admit the truth. Another large component of the Pigman's character was the elderly Italian grandfather of one of Zindel's few childhood friends; the man pressed his own wine and regularly invited Zindel and his family to his Sunday picnics. A third aspect of the character was drawn from a story Zindel heard from an actor in Houston about an old man in Boston who collected pigs.

The author believes that a fourth component of his central character was the father he lacked in his own life—what he imagined a father should be.[16]

Zindel derived much of the strange and antagonistic behavior of John's and Lorraine's parents from his own unhappy relationships with his mother and father. Despite this, however, he dedicated *The Pigman* to them in a cryptic postscript—"For the Boy and Girl of Stapleton"—naming the town where they grew up. The dedication might be simply an honor the author bestowed on his mother and father, or it might imply that their problems (like those of John's and Lorraine's parents) were related to the fact that they never really grew up.

The critical reception of *The Pigman* was as positive as Donelson and Nilsen's later evaluation. The *School Library Journal* said it was "intensely moving" and alluded to its facility for provoking discussion.[17] *Horn Book* called it "a now book," going on to state that few books are "as cruelly truthful about the human condition."[18] The *New York Times Book Review* sounded a note that has become familiar in later criticism of Zindel novels: *The Pigman* possessed "the right combination of the preposterous and the sensible," although John Weston, the reviewer, felt that the author was "patronizing his readers by spelling out the moral" at the end.[19] And *Publishers Weekly* waxed poetic in its praise after pointing out the ground-breaking nature of the novel; its reviewer said that she felt "like the watcher of the skies when a new planet swims into his ken."[20]

Not surprisingly, when Zindel's second novel, *My Darling, My Hamburger,* was published two years later, it was measured against *The Pigman*—and some critics found it wanting. In his second story, Zindel was treading on dangerous ground because he was writing about teenage sex—a subject that at the time was taboo in young adult literature. He was, however, very careful to keep within the bounds of accepted norms. Except for an occasional kiss, all the sexual activity takes place offstage. In addition, he employed the third-person omniscient narrative to tell the story instead of the more intimate first-person narrative he had used in *The Pigman.*

My Darling, My Hamburger revolves around the interrelation-
ships of four teenagers.[21] Sean, a sensitive and confused adolescent, has a father whose values center on making money and
getting away with as much as possible. His equally confused girlfriend, Liz, is constantly at odds with an overprotective mother
and a suspicious stepfather. Contrasted with this couple are Dennis and Maggie (Liz's close friend), who are modest, innocent,
caring, and self-conscious. Both Dennis and Maggie have parents
who are veritable models of understanding and love.

Until Sean met Liz, he had looked at life as "one huge pathetic
waste" (p. 18). Now he thinks he is deeply in love. But when Sean
pressures Liz to sleep with him, it is too much for her to handle,
so she temporarily breaks off their romance. Dennis and Maggie,
on the other hand, are so afraid of physical contact that when
Dennis one night attempts a tentative awkward kiss, Maggie
nervously trots out the line her sex education teacher advised
girls to use "when things get out of control": "I think we'd better
go get a hamburger" (p. 6).

In the meantime, Liz—who is still emotionally involved with
Sean—goes to the Winter Starlight Dance with semidelinquent
Rod Gittens just to make Sean jealous. She is in over her head,
however, when Rod tries to molest her. A vigilant and protective
Sean saves her from this attack, and they become a twosome once
again. When Liz's mother and stepfather berate her for staying
out late, she rebelliously decides to give in to Sean's sexual demands. She later discovers she has become pregnant. A frightened
Sean first agrees to marry her, but his hard-nosed father con-
vinces him that Liz should have an abortion. Maggie helps her
terrified friend get the then illegal operation, and when medical
complications set in, she saves Liz's life by getting help for her.
Although Maggie had had to break a date with Dennis to help
Liz with the abortion, she and he part amicably after graduation
and promise to keep in touch. Sean and Liz, however, are left
deep in guilt and confusion, bearing lifetime scars from their
ordeal. The moral is clear: Liz's and Sean's failure to take responsibility for their actions has shattered their lives, whereas

Dennis and Maggie emerge with slightly bruised feelings but wiser and stronger because of their accountability.

Zindel modeled the character of Maggie on a girl who wanted to date him when he was in high school. She was overweight and had a mother who successfully taught her to overcome the handicap of her obesity by developing her personality. Liz was based on a very beautiful young woman Zindel dated when he was in college. She looked, he says, like Marilyn Monroe and behaved recklessly. Like Eugene Dingman's girlfriend in Zindel's most recent adult novel, she used to leave him at 2:00 A.M. after a date, and then walk in her house and out the back door into another boy's car. Like Liz, she also had an illegal abortion.

The source of Sean's character was a boy in one of Zindel's chemistry classes when he taught at a Staten Island high school. The boy, Zindel remembers, appeared to have all the right things going for him—family, wealth, intelligence, and popularity—but Zindel always felt it was only appearance. Dennis, on the other hand, was based on a "dopey" boy Zindel met while he lived in the castle where he met John; the boy reminded him of himself when he was in high school.[22]

Although the novel was well received by teenage readers, reviewers were disappointed. (Zindel says that *My Darling, My Hamburger* is still the novel of his that is most read by black students.) *Horn Book* reviewer Diane Farrell—who also had evaluated *The Pigman* for the magazine—focused her criticism on the stereotyping of characters.[23] The *Bulletin of the Center for Children's Books* agreed with Farrell, saying that "the characters seem to move stiffly to adapt to a pattern."[24] And *Library Journal* reviewer Marilyn Singer criticized the novel for "copping out" on the sexual issues raised in the story. Singer also identified the reasons teenage readers might like the novel: the book was "skillfully written" and contained "natural, entertaining and often funny dialogue and description."[25]

A year later, Zindel returned to the first-person narrative and published *I Never Loved Your Mind,* a zany story that uses the trappings of the 1960s to usher in with subdued fanfare the "Me

Decade" of the 1970s. The novel was born from Zindel's frustrations and disillusionments with teaching and his increasing alienation from the youth culture.[26]

Dewey Daniels, a self-conscious, pretentious, but innocent high school dropout, has opted out of a place he found irrelevant and landed a job in a hospital as an assistant in the inhalation therapy department.[27] In the style and voice of *Catcher in the Rye*'s Holden Caulfield (Zindel claims the similarity was inadvertent), he tells about his relationship with a young nurse named Yvette Goethals. On his first day at work, Dewey faints at the sight of blood and wakes up to find Yvette helping him. The young nurse, whom Dewey immediately notices is blessed with "a commendable frontal insulation for the respiratory cage" (p. 14), is a vegetarian and acid-tongued. Like characters in Zindel's other young adult novels and adult plays—and like Zindel's own mother—Yvette steals petty items liberally from the hospital.[28] On a date with her, Dewey learns that she is living with a rock band. He is curious about the lifestyle of the band, but the curiosity turns to shock when he visits Yvette in her apartment and finds her vacuuming in the nude. At her urging, he sheds his own clothes, graduates to massages, and finally engages in lovemaking (offstage). That experience sets long-winded and little-experienced Dewey into a "love tailspin." Yvette, however, does not reciprocate, and Dewey soon discovers that she has been evicted from her apartment, along with her rock friends. At a party that turns into a free-for-all, he and Yvette part. Dewey rejects her hedonistic life-style, leaves the hospital, and decides to prepare for medical school. He has decided that he is not going to "give civilization a kick in the behind because [he] might need an appendectomy sometime" (p. 181).

In this often funny satire of the sixties youth culture, Zindel no doubt offended some of his intended readers. But some critics reacted as if the author had given *them* "a kick in the behind." "Relentlessly flip" and "moralizing" was the best the *Library Journal* could say about the story.[29] "Ugly hopelessness" was *Publishers Weekly*'s verdict.[30] The *New York Times Book Review* critic Josh Greenfield said it was an "adult con." But what he called "a sweet and sour mash of old boy-meets-girl pulp poured into a contemporary hippy flask"[31] was actually for Zindel an expression of the fact that he "didn't really fit into the sub-culture." In 1968, one of Zindel's friends had given him a house to live in in Taos, New Mexico, where for six months he was surrounded by newly formed youth communes permeated by unconventional values: drugs, free sex, and macrobiotic diets. It was a discomfiting experience for him. Soon after Zindel returned to "civilization," he needed an appendectomy, and, he says, he was grateful "that a traditional doctor was working on him rather than someone at Hot Springs commune."[32]

Both Yvette's and Dewey's characters were rooted in students whom Zindel had taught. Yvette was based on a risk-taking, troubled orphan whom the author befriended. Dewey's original was "nasty and a little preppy and was probably compensating for some of his inadequacies."[33] Zindel added a lot of himself to this student, whom he barely knew; he gave him the same naïveté about Yvette's psychedelic world that had once characterized his own approach to the youth culture.

Six years elapsed between *I Never Loved Your Mind* and Zindel's next young adult novel, *Pardon Me, You're Stepping on My Eyeball.* In the interim, he wrote plays and a children's picture book entitled *I Love My Mother*—a story that sugarcoated his ambivalent feelings toward his larger-than-life mother.

"Larger than life" is an apt description of how Zindel began to look at his own life, and the two teenage novels he wrote after *I Never Loved Your Mind* illustrate the intensity of his self-reflection. *Pardon Me, You're Stepping on My Eyeball* and *Confessions of a Teenage Baboon* are highly personal stories that not only expose the depth of Zindel's feelings toward his parents but also focus on a theme of great importance to him—self-worth.

Written in the third person, *Pardon Me* is about two disturbed teenagers who find themselves "prisoners" in their school's group-therapy class.[34] Fifteen-year-old "Marsh" Mellow supposedly has two parents—his mother, whom he calls "Schizoid Suzie" because of her alcoholism and denigration of Marsh, and his father, whom he labels "Paranoid Pete." In truth, his father died in an accident in which Marsh played a part. But he cannot confront the truth, so he hides his father's ashes under his bed and walks around with a pet baby raccoon in his pocket. And he lies compulsively—about girls he knows and about his father whom he glorifies. Edna Shinglebox has two real parents who push her into everything (especially meeting boys). They think she is hopelessly deficient in everything.

As Marsh unfolds his story to Edna through a series of letters supposedly written by his father, she gradually realizes the truth and knows that Marsh must come to grips with it. Shedding her insularity, she consults a local psychic who tells her that Marsh must first purge himself through some symbolic act. After a wild party in which Marsh's raccoon dies in a fire, Marsh and Edna flee—with Pete's ashes—on an impulsive midnight ride to Washington, D.C., where Marsh is supposedly going to meet his father at a mental institution. Their car crashes, however, and in a climactic conclusion, Edna pushes the ashes off a cliff and Marsh sets off a rocket he and his father had bought just before the accident that killed Pete. Edna successfully declares her independence from her meddling parents, and Marsh—in a cathartic eruption of fireworks, a symbolic act of repentance—frees himself from his self-imposed prison.

Zindel got the idea for an act of repentance from "a gypsy-like man who loved the opera" with whom he shared his guilt feelings about his recently deceased mother.[35] The man told the author that he was like the Pigman who could not accept the reality of his wife's death, and he suggested that Zindel take a copy of his first novel to his mother's grave and bury it. Although Zindel never did that, he applied the therapeutic idea to writing about Marsh's catharsis. Zindel dedicated *Pardon Me* to John Foster, the man who had introduced him to the excitements of the New York City theater but who later became involved in drugs and burned to death in a fire. Perhaps the dedication itself was another use of a symbolic act, helping Zindel accept the tragedy of his friend's death.

Zindel says the inspiration for the characters in *Pardon Me* stemmed from his own life. Edna, he claims, is himself as a teenager trying to forge a self-identity and free himself from a dominating mother. Marsh's struggles, too, are Zindel's: the attempts to accept a childhood and adolescence without a father and to cope with his mother's death. Further, the author says that even the midnight ride to Washington mirrors an episode in his troubled adolescence—his flight to Miami.

The idea of giving Marsh a raccoon as a consoling companion was lifted from an experience the author had while leading a week-long workshop at Ohio Wesleyan College. Zindel noticed a student in the class who carried a small raccoon in his pocket, and although he never found out why he did this, he made use of the incident in *Pardon Me*.[36]

Pardon Me was the first Zindel novel to win a place on the Best Books for Young Adults annual list—and some critics were also impressed with the unusual story. *Publishers Weekly* called the novel "a classy combination of outrageous happenings, comedy, tragedy and compassion."[37] The *New York Times Book Review* praised the "supercharged imagination" behind the story.[38] The *School Library Journal*, on the other hand, criticized the novel for its abundance of clichés and predictability,[39] and *Booklist* faulted it for stereotyping its adult characters.[40]

Also mixed were the reviews of Zindel's next novel, *Confessions of a Teenage Baboon*, published one year after *Pardon Me*. Again, the *School Library Journal* was very critical, citing the bleakness and the black comedy permeating the story where "every character is sick, physically or mentally." Although Shirley Wilton, the reviewer, implicitly approved of Zindel's message—"in a world of corruption and absurdity, the individual can affirm his own integrity and responsibility"—she concluded by saying "it takes more work than it's worth to sort it all out."[41] Yet *Publishers Weekly* believed it not only was worth sorting all out but was "a work of art—moving, as well as funny."[42]

Zindel says that writing this novel almost gave him a nervous breakdown because of its parallels to his own life.[43] Sixteen-year-old Chris Boyd is "the teenage baboon" narrator of the story.[44] He and his mother, Helen, an itinerant nurse, live wherever she can find work. Chris's father died in Mexico years before, leaving his son an oversized Chesterfield coat as his legacy. Thirty-year-old shiploader Lloyd Dipardi hires Helen to care for his terminally ill mother whom he both hates and loves. When Helen and Chris move in, they discover that Lloyd has developed around him a coterie of alienated teenagers whom he has befriended. Each week, late-night parties are held at the house, and Lloyd's young friends gradually break down barriers they have erected between themselves and the outside world.

Chris, however, does not get along with Lloyd because the sixteen-year-old sees the shiploader as an alcoholic, egotistical tyrant lording over his teenage hangers-on. Nor does Helen get along with Lloyd because the nurse thinks he is insensitive to his mother's needs—and a threat to her authority. Lloyd's hostility to his mother can be traced to a childhood incident when his mother found him playing a sexual game with a toy bear and threatened to burn off his penis. Since then, Lloyd has spent his life unsuccessfully trying to establish his manhood. He has a weapon against Chris, however: he knows the boy has a domineering mother and an unhealthy tie to his dead father. With the help of Rosemary, one of his alienated teenagers, the shiploader induces Chris to trust him and urges him to start accepting responsibility for his own life—advice Dipardi himself has been unable to follow. In the aftermath of one of Lloyd's riotous parties, Helen angrily quits her job, and dragging Chris with her, she leaves the Dipardi house—but without Chris's treasured Chesterfield coat. Against his mother's wishes, Chris returns to retrieve the coat and, to his horror, witnesses in quick succession the death of Lloyd's mother, Lloyd being beaten up by policemen, and finally Lloyd's suicide by shotgun. These shattering events jolt Chris into freeing himself from the suffocating hold of his mother and dead father. As the story ends, he and Rosemary hold hands and are able to think about their future together.

Zindel had never actually met the person from whom he derived the character of Lloyd Dipardi. While he was teaching in high school, a story appeared in a Staten Island newspaper concerning a "rednecky, alcoholic" shipworker who was arrested for having sex with twenty teenagers. A jealous boyfriend of one of the girls informed the police, and the man was arrested on a morals charge.

But, Zindel says, the judge was paid off, and the shipworker was free to continue his activities. On this skeletal incident, Zindel superimposed his own adolescent struggle to free himself from the hold of his mother and the pain of a missing father.[45] Lloyd and Chris both are alter egos of sorts for Zindel. Lloyd has a dying mother and no father and represents the half of Zindel whose past has so maimed him that he cannot begin again; Chris is the half that signifies the potential to change. Therefore, by having Lloyd commit suicide (after being beaten by police—Zindel's father's occupation), Zindel was killing off his neurosis about his parents. In witnessing Lloyd's death, Chris becomes the survivor. And it is likely that Rosemary's support and love at the story's conclusion represents the support and love Zindel's wife, Bonnie, provided when the author was coming to terms with his mother's death and his sudden fame when he won the Pulitzer Prize.

Concluding his first decade of writing young adult novels, Zindel in 1978 published his sixth story for teenagers—*The Undertaker's Gone Bananas*. This story broke new ground for the author in many ways. It was his first mystery-adventure novel; it was the first in which the heroes' parents are happily married; and it was the first in which the main characters are focused not just on themselves but also on trying to right a wrong.

Bobby and Lauri live in the same apartment building and have been close friends ever since Lauri saved Bobby from prosecution after a block party fight.[46] A rebellious adolescent always wary of pretension, Bobby is suspicious of all authority except his model parents. When Mr. Hulka and his wife move next door, Bobby quickly discovers he is an undertaker and begins to spy on his strange habits. One day, Bobby believes he sees his new neighbor stabbing his wife, so he calls the police. But they find nothing, and Bobby appears foolish. He enlists Lauri's help to find out what is going on, and together they follow Hulka to his funeral home and then to a nearby bridge where they see him throw a suitcase into the water below. As the mystery deepens, Lauri— who has for many years lacked self-confidence and security after witnessing a fire in which a neighbor was killed—realizes this is not just another of Bobby's attempts to help her. A real crime has been perpetrated, and she and Bobby may solve it. As they close in on the truth, Hulka traps them briefly in Bobby's apartment, but they escape. A headlong car chase ends in the villain's capture. Bobby and Lauri, kissing each other, exit in the police car as heroes.

The nature of the critical reaction to this relatively lighthearted novel indicated how different *The Undertaker's Gone Bananas* was from the two confessional novels preceding it. "A zany farce," the *New York Times Book Review* called it.[47] *Horn Book* said it "was thoroughly entertaining and filled with genuine humor,"[48] and *Booklist* singled out for praise the novel's "appealing characters."[49] It was like a sigh of comic relief after the author had purged so much pain about himself and his family.

Yet the source of Mr. Hulka was far from comic relief for Zindel. After their wedding ceremony in London, the Zindels had returned to the United States and moved into a north New Jersey apartment overlooking the Hudson River. Within a few weeks, a "dashing, ostentatious" man, his wife, and his children moved into the apartment next to the Zindels'. The author discovered that the man, who told Zindel he was a mortician, collected dollhouses with hand-carved figures inside and antique men's Victorian toilet kits. While his wife was preparing dinner one evening, Zindel answered a knock at the door and found his new neighbor standing on the threshold holding miniature clay figures involved "in unconventional sexual acts." Zindel was beginning to question this person's taste, when the undertaker gave the author a paper bag that held a gun handle attached to a large clay penis. Frightened and angry now, Zindel asked him to leave. Zindel was so upset by this bizarre man that he and his wife moved to Connecticut. Zindel says that Bobby and Lauri are actually he and Bonnie trying to rid themselves of the influence of their former neighbor. He also freely borrowed from life images in other novels. For instance, Bobby's rebelliousness, down to his getting into trouble with police at a block party, is taken from the original of John Conlan in *The Pigman*. And Lauri follows in the mold of Lorraine and Maggie, girls who are insecure, afraid of life, vulnerable, and dependable.[50]

In the six young adult novels Zindel wrote between 1968 and 1978, there appears to be a thematic progression in the author's concerns. He begins with the notion of one's taking personal responsibility for one's actions, then turns to the quest for self-confidence and self-understanding, and finally focuses on love. After ending *The Undertaker's Gone Bananas* with Bobby and Lauri kissing, Zindel decided to write a sequel to *The Pigman* which would develop the romantic relationship between John and Lorraine; he titled it *The Pigman's Legacy*.

The story begins one and a half years after John and Lorraine's tragic encounter with Mr. Pignati.[51] Again, the two narrate the story in alternate chapters. Expecting to find Mr. Pignati's house deserted, they revisit the place after missing their bus stop on the way home from school. To their surprise, they find an old man living there. The man first calls himself Gus and then reveals he is a once-proud colonel who is sick and lonely; Gus is actually his dog's name. In the games he plays to reach out to them, he reminds them of the Pigman's loneliness. To keep the old man from starving, the two teens secretly bring food from their homes for him. And they invite a friend, Dolly Racinski—the cleaning lady in their school cafeteria—to befriend the colonel. As it becomes clear that the old man is dying, they all decide to have a last fling gambling in Atlantic City. At first, they win a great deal, but John compulsively continues until they lose not only their winnings but all their money. During this fiasco, Lorraine openly proclaims her love for John, giving him the courage and support to face up to his gambling sickness and the harm he has done. Then the colonel loses consciousness, and they rush him to a hospital. In a frenzied and moving climax involving Dolly, John, Lorraine, and Gus the dog, the colonel dies, and John reciprocates Lorraine's declaration of love.

The path to romance traveled by John and Lorraine from the beginning of *The Pigman* to the end of the *Legacy* reflects a comparable road traveled by Zindel himself. He learned to accept responsibility for his actions, worked through his character weaknesses and phobias, and emerged strengthened and committed to a relationship with the woman he loved.

By design, the sequel was derivative of *The Pigman*. Most reviews alluded to this, but only one judged the successor to be greatly inferior. The *School Library Journal* said *The Pigman*'s "strong characterization, credibility and skilled story development" was missing from the sequel.[52] Most reviews, however, were very positive. "A rousing adventure yarn" and "a surprising, beautiful and even profound story," praised the *New York Times Book Review*. Zindel, the review claimed, "has wrapped his sequel around its precursor, returning to old themes but enlarging and deepening them."[53] *Booklist* added that "the more upbeat denouement" would be welcomed by teen readers.[54] And the novel was placed on the Best Books for Young Adults list. (A controversy about the authorship of *The Pigman's Legacy* emerged a year after its publication. For a brief discussion of this, see chapter 3.)

The Girl Who Wanted a Boy, published in 1981 while Zindel and his family were living in California, is by most critical standards his least substantial and least successful young adult novel. It lacks a believable heroine, a credible plot, and the humor to offset his blatant character stereotypes. A mechanically inclined fifteen-year-old named Sibella has never dated, but she decides it is time to change.[55] Her older sister, Maureen, who is living with a boyfriend, has bequeathed her slow-starting sister a book entitled *How to Pick up Boys*. Sibella digests the information in this short book and wonders how to apply her new knowledge. One day, she sees a picture of an auto mechanic who appeals to her; she seeks him out and professes her love. Dan, the lucky man, at first rejects her onslaught because he thinks she is merely young and confused. But when she offers to spend her savings on a van to free him from his dead-end job, he changes his mind. He accepts the van, makes love to her, and leaves. Depressed at Dan's rejection, Sibella becomes suicidal, but with her mother's support, she draws on an inner strength and comes to view the incident as a learning experience rather than a personal rebuff.

Oddly enough, the inspiration to write this novel had more to do with the source Zindel used for Dan than with his model for Sibella. When the author and his family were living in California, Mary Beth—the sixteen-year-old adopted daughter of his sister,

Betty, and her husband—visited the Zindels. While there, she invited a boyfriend to the house, and they swam together in Zindel's pool. Engaging them in conversation, Zindel questioned Mary Beth's boyfriend about his life ambitions and discovered that his entire aspirations centered on owning a large-wheel truck and driving it to Daytona Beach. What would happen, Zindel thought, if he were to create a Maggie-type character with a scientific bent (like Tillie in *Gamma Rays*) and have her fall in love with such "an empty-headed" guy?[56]

The resulting book, *The Girl Who Wanted a Boy*, he dedicated to Mary Beth and her half-brother, Eddie, but Zindel says that in no way does she resemble Sibella. Terming the story "a pot-boiler," Zindel acknowledges that he wrote it quickly, primarily for money, and that the characterizations are "very thin."[57] Most reviewers agreed. With the exception of *Publishers Weekly*, which found the novel "profoundly moving and humorous,"[58] *The Girl Who Wanted a Boy* was widely criticized. *Booklist* said that it "was not as cohesive or affecting" as his previous novels;[59] the *School Library Journal* called it a "dismal novel";[60] and the *New York Times Book Review* termed it "embarrassing."[61]

Zindel returned to his tried and true *Pigman* formula of storytelling in his next novel, *Harry and Hortense at Hormone High*, published in 1984.[62] It is narrated by two classmates (like John and Lorraine) whose close friendship has budding romantic overtones. They meet new student Jason Rohr, a tall, mysterious, majestic-looking boy who fancies himself a Greek god trying to save the world. Against their better judgment, they take an interest in him. After some amateur sleuthing, they discover that the "god" lives in a ramshackle hut with a poor aunt who can barely speak English. Jason cultivates Harry and Hortense's friendship and tells them he is thousands of years old—he is Icarus, half god, half man, who "can help people find the god in themselves" (p. 49). (In Greek mythology, Icarus—against his father's wishes—flew too close to the sun and fell to his death when his waxen artificial wings melted.) Harry and Hortense are incredulous, but they are nonetheless drawn to the boy because the two are in search of real heroes. To find out the truth about

Jason, they break into the school office and rifle through his records. When he was six years old, they discover, his father murdered his mother and then killed himself.

Meanwhile, Jason has become increasingly disliked at school because of his pretense of divinity. When classmates kill his beloved Great Dane, Darwin, Jason scribbles graffiti all over the school, and authorities send him back to the sanatorium from which he came. But he escapes, with Harry and Hortense's help, returns to school, and takes over the microphone system to preach his message of deliverance to his former classmates. Next day, he plants stolen dynamite in the school office and, attached to a hang glider powered by a lawn-mower engine, barricades himself on top of the roof. As Jason takes off, the dynamite blows up the office, but his amateur machine fails, and Jason plunges to his death in the river below. Badly shaken, Harry and Hortense struggle to find some purpose in this tragedy. They resolve that their friend's delusions will give them the strength and inspiration to fight against the world's evils.

Zindel created Hortense in Lorraine's mold—introspective, a bit frightened, and very sensitive to people's feelings. Hortense complements Harry, whom Zindel endowed with a mixture of a devilishness and naïveté. Both the hero and the heroine were created in the author's image because Zindel wrote the novel to communicate his strong feelings about contemporary civilization. He believes our society is mired in the school of realism; it lacks the spirituality and heroes to keep the values of civilization alive and transmit them from one generation to the next. The myths of ancient Greece, Zindel says, portrayed human nature in its purest form and put us in touch with our basic instincts which are "very holy." Zindel used Harry and Hortense's disillusionment with the materialism permeating their society to represent his own alienation. He intended their encounter with Jason and the renewal of their life after his death to reflect his own attempt to regain what he calls "the emotional center of humanity" and to turn his life toward a worthy direction.[63]

Many critics, however, found the book to be considerably less meaningful. Patricia Campbell, writing in the *Wilson Library*

Bulletin, called the story "preposterous" and "a peculiar book that lacks Zindel's redeeming wit." She also noted that the legacy left by Jason was so amorphous that it was practically meaningless.[64] Although the *School Library Journal* disagreed with Campbell about the novel's wit, its reviewer, Cathryn Male, agreed that Zindel did not make sufficiently clear what his message was. "Unfortunately," she wrote, "the novel parodies the underlying mythical tragedy rather than highlighting it."[65] *Publishers Weekly* concurred. Even *Horn Book*'s review, which praised the novel, mentioned its lack of clarity. The book's "smart-cracking surrealistic style," the review said, "defends the story against apathy or despair."[66] But Zindel wanted the novel to inspire his young readers, not leave them with apathy or despair; he wanted the book's power to come from its theme, not from its "smart-cracking style."

Zindel's most recent young adult novel, *The Amazing and Death-Defying Diary of Eugene Dingman,* was published in 1987. It is a farce with a moral—a story that explores the importance of self-esteem, a recurrent theme in Zindel's work.

Eugene begins his diary just before he leaves home for a summer job at an Adirondacks resort, the Lake Henry Hotel. Six years earlier, his father ran off with a "statuesque secretary," and recently his lonely, frustrated mother has begun a romantic relationship with her new boarder. On arriving at the hotel, Eugene finds that his fellow employees resemble a subhuman life form; their need for self-gratification and their greed appear limitless. Eugene also discovers that his customers are a motley group of eccentrics whose public behavior is at best embarrassing. Letters from his mother, his father, the woman his father is living with, and his sister, Penelope, who hates his father, provide him with domestic news. Eugene's diary soon focuses on his two main concerns of the summer: Della, a beautiful waitress with whom he becomes obsessed, and her boyfriend, Bunker, who is the hotel's broiler chef and whose mean streak is turned on Eugene when he tries to become Della's friend. Each diary entry—which begins with a trivia date, a literary quotation, or a headline from Eugene's *National Enquirer*–like hometown newspaper—chronicles his increasing frustration over Della and his fear of Bunker. Taking her aunt's advice to be "selfish in the best sense" (p. 88), Della wants to play the field. And Bunker—ignored by Della and jealous of Eugene—becomes more threatening, nearly drowning the young diarist by buzzing Eugene's canoe with an airboat and causing it to capsize.

Eugene consults with Mahatma, a Hindu guru and hotel groundskeeper. Mahatma lives with some of his countrymen in a separate house because no one can stand the smell of their curry. Mahatma tells Eugene that before he can expect someone to love him, he must love himself. "The secret of life is reversal. . . . the answer is always the opposite of what you think" (p. 108). Disappointed by his father, who breaks a promise to visit him, and disillusioned by Della, who first lies to him and then tells him he lives in a fantasy world, Eugene is shocked into taking control of his disintegrating life. At the hotel, he refuses a supervisor's order to serve poisoned food to a customer his boss is mad at and is fired on the spot. As he is taking his final canoe ride in the lake, Bunker again confronts him. This time, however, Eugene remembers the guru's advice and rows straight toward Bunker's airboat, catching the bully off guard and forcing *him* to capsize. "In the midst of winter," Eugene quotes Camus at the end of the novel, "I finally learned that there was in me an invincible summer." His last entry is: "Eugene Dingman born" (p. 214).

And, of course, the author, too, is reborn—for of all his teenage protagonists, Eugene Dingman is the flimsiest disguise for Zindel himself. Eugene's family is a mirror image of Zindel's. The author was sixteen when he began a job as a waiter at an Adirondacks hotel. Della is a composite of girls the author dated, with a large part of her character derived from a girl Zindel knew at Wagner College—the same person who was the inspiration for Liz in *My Darling, My Hamburger*. "All my characters learn a lesson—and I learn the lesson along with them," Zindel has said.[67] Eugene loses his innocence and at the same time begins to control his life. With Eugene, his creator found "an invincible summer" deep within himself.

In each of his young adult novels, Zindel has adhered to the ten-part formula given at the beginning of this chapter. He has, in fact, repeated plot action and character development to such a degree that one might justifiably claim that his stories are derivative of one another. Why is this so? Despite his theorizing about what teenagers want to read, how to write for them, and what he wants to teach them, Zindel—at a basic level—is attempting to solve his own problems. In writing about Chris's father abandoning his family and leaving an oversized overcoat as his legacy to his son *(Confessions of a Teenage Baboon)* or in portraying Marsh's fixation with his dead father's ashes *(Pardon Me)*, Zindel is first of all coming to grips with his fatherless childhood. In writing about Edna's overprotective, domineering mother *(Pardon Me)* or Chris's overbearing mother *(Confessions)*, the author is trying to resolve his ambivalence about his own eccentric mother. And finally in the attempts of Marsh, Edna, Eugene, Chris, John, and Lorraine to overcome the effects of a broken family and forge a self-identity, Zindel is portraying his own efforts to do the same. It is this overriding concern with the pain of his childhood and his adolescence that leads to the repetitiveness of his stories.

His preoccupation with solving his own problems, however, also accounts for his novels' special appeal to teenagers. The stories are immersed in the essence of adolescence—the definition of oneself against one's immediate environment. Given the novels' sharp, believable dialogue, their unpretentious teenage heroes and heroines, their strong satire of adult society, and their conflicts involving self and family which almost all teenagers have to confront during their adolescence, it makes little difference to his readers that Zindel is writing the same book again and again, or that he is working through his own arrested adolescence. Zindel's career as a young adult novelist is a classic example of a writer's need and that of his audience complementing one another perfectly.

3. *To Take a Dare:* Collaborations and Other Prose

Not all of Zindel's fiction has fit into the neat patterns and set principles the author has followed in most of his young adult novels. He has lent his name to two stories for teenagers he helped others write—*A Star for the Latecomer* and *To Take a Dare,* both of which differ greatly from Zindel's own work. He has also written a picture book for children, *I Love My Mother,* and a sexually explicit adult novel, *When a Darkness Falls;* these two demonstrate his willingness to take chances with form and substance and different audiences.

Under the byline of Bonnie Zindel and Paul Zindel, *A Star for the Latecomer* was published by Harper & Row in 1980. It is less frenetically paced and more controlled than Zindel's other novels. On the one hand, it lacks the rich metaphor and leavening humor common to most of his young adult fiction. On the other, the novel contains a component missing from his previous work: an adult antagonist who is sympathetically and realistically portrayed. Seventeen-year-old Brooke Hillary looks back at her life during the year just past.[1] She has been studying dance at a special school for the performing arts, primarily because her ambitious mother pushed her into it. Deep down, Brooke knows she is in the wrong place, and she resents being there. The focus of the story, however, is on Brooke's relationship with her mother, who is slowly and painfully dying of cancer. Mixed with her deep resentments is an equally deep love and empathy for her sick parent, which leaves her feeling confused and anxious. When her mother finally dies, Brooke decides to leave the school. She buries her dancing shoes and dress with her mother and silently says a farewell: "You told me that I have choices in life, and for the first time in my life, I know what you mean. I feel free" (p. 184).

As many of the novel's reviewers have pointed out, it was obvious that this story was not from the pen of Paul Zindel. "Whatever one expects of a Zindel novel, this is not it," the *School Library Journal* asserted. "There are no drunk mothers, wayward fathers and 'off the wall' kids trying to find one another."[2] *Booklist* also noted the difference and said "it's a relatively low-key (borderline sentimental) junior novel . . . more a character study than a story of action. It may attract a slightly different audience from that of Zindel's previous books."[3] Most of the reviews criticized the message-laden conclusion of the story, but they also praised the moving scenes between Brooke and her terminally ill mother.

According to Zindel's editor, Charlotte Zolotow, and Zindel himself, the novel was written by Bonnie Zindel. It was, however, originally submitted to Harper by Paul Zindel instead of by his wife because he believed it would have a better chance of being considered than if Bonnie sent it. It was only when Zolotow asked Zindel for a rewrite that he revealed that it was his wife's novel and said that he would work with her on a revision. His contribution to the novel was to help his wife structure and focus the story.[4]

Like most of Zindel's own young adult novels, this book contains a considerable element of autobiography. Bonnie Zindel initially was trained to be a dancer, and her mother was a major influence in the decision. When she was seventeen, she lost her mother to cancer after a protracted struggle with the disease. Her protagonist, Brooke, learns an important lesson about herself, and Bonnie Zindel learned it along with her.

Zindel's role in writing *To Take a Dare* was another matter. Crescent Dragonwagon, an established picture-book writer and daughter of Charlotte Zolotow, was having trouble finishing a young adult novel based loosely on her own life. In late March 1980 she decided to ask Zindel for help because she admired his writing and because she knew of his collaboration with his wife. She had also just reviewed *A Star for the Latecomer* for the *Arkansas Gazette* and was impressed with the book. Without her mother's knowledge, she contacted Zindel, and he agreed to help.[5] Zindel says he had known of her previous writing and felt that her work was "brazen, tough, and beautifully written."[6] He had never met her before, however.

Why did Zindel decide to help someone he did not know? At the time, he was living in California and was heavily involved in writing screenplays, which itself is collaborative in nature. Zindel says that during this period he felt "indefatigable and could do no wrong."[7] He also remembers the collaboration with Dragonwagon as constituting an antidote to boredom and a professional challenge to pull out the story Dragonwagon was trying to write. After they had begun their collaborative effort, they told Harper & Row what they were doing. Despite some misgivings, Harper signed them to a contract. Crescent Dragonwagon writes that Zindel provided support and help with structuring her novel; he was "a sounding board and a cheerleader" who contributed "gentle criticism and lavish praise." With this help and Zindel's promise that he would finish the story if she could not, Dragonwagon triumphantly completed *To Take a Dare* after writing three drafts.[8]

One of the suggestions Zindel made to Dragonwagon was to make the story less autobiographical than she had originally intended it to be. She accepted this advice, and she says it made the novel more effective.[9] "Because the book's setting is autogeographical," Dragonwagon writes in her preface to the novel, "some readers may assume that the characters too are drawn straight from real life. In this, however, they would be mistaken. . . . They have their only real life in this book."

The story is about thirteen-year-old Chrysta Perretti who runs away from her Illinois suburb because she cannot deal with her difficult parents and because she is confused by the physical and emotional changes taking place in her.[10] After two years of misadventures, she stops running and settles down in a small Arkansas town, working as a chef. She falls in love with Luke, a tall, handsome young folk singer who cares for her deeply. She also takes on the responsibility of being a mother to a boy named Dare—a runaway like herself. The ups and downs of this relationship give Chrysta the insight to understand how her mother felt. Dare continually flouts Chrysta's rules and authority, so she gives him an ultimatum: either abide by the rules she has set or leave. When Dare's undependable father disappoints the boy by not visiting him on his birthday, Dare finally understands the true situation. But he cannot accept either himself or Chrysta's love and authority, so he leaves for good. Although deeply hurt by Dare's decision, Chrysta draws closer to Luke and begins to believe "she can make her own happy endings" (p. 246). And finally she feels able to call her parents and try to make up for the lost years.

After the novel was published, Dragonwagon quotes Zindel as saying, "Well, sure, *To Take a Dare* has weak points. But you know, you did write it out of your blood and guts and heart; you did write it honestly. And that's what comes across most strongly to readers."[11] Many reviewers, however, did not agree. The *School Library Journal* criticized its "semi-explicit sex and strong language" and complained it "was loaded with messages."[12] Similarly, the *New York Times Book Review* said the story was "as moralistic as any Hollywood romance of the Production Code era," even though the book "exuded a nervy self-confidence" that would appeal to teenagers.[13] The *English Journal* faulted the novel for nonexistent character development and cast the story's message into sarcastic terms: "If you run away and suffer a bit, things will all work out."[14]

The collaboration also led to a controversy over *The Pigman's Legacy,* which Zindel had published in 1980. At the American Library Association's annual conference in 1983, Alleen Pace Nilsen, a young adult literature specialist and coauthor of a history of the genre, gave a speech entitled "Bottoms Up in YA Literature" in which she attacked the tendency among young adult novelists to accept and exploit the stereotypes and clichés of our time. She singled out the idea of "love as a cure-all" and criticized Dragonwagon for basing the resolution of Chrysta's problems upon her reliance on Luke. Quoting one of Patricia Campbell's columns in the *Wilson Library Bulletin,* which had focused on young adult novels about disturbed teenagers, she said the message Dragonwagon left with the reader was unfortunate: "Nutty girls should look around for a stalwart boy to save them."[15]

The controversy aroused by her speech, however, did not concern her criticism of Dragonwagon's novel. It arose from a relatively brief reference she made to Dominic Lagotta, a twenty-six-year-old former neighbor of Zindel's whom the author had hired to help write *The Pigman's Legacy.* The *New York Times* reported that Lagotta claimed he had written the novel's first draft and that the final version contained "75% of his plot and 22% of the draft word-for-word." Lagotta was paid $10,000 for his work, the newspaper report said, and now he was suing for $200,000, a percentage of royalties, recognition as coauthor, and $1 million in damages.[16] (The suit was settled out of court with the provision that none of the parties would reveal the settlement or discuss it publicly.)

Nilsen claimed in her speech that this episode "left a lot of us with a strange little after-taste in our mouths." She was further upset by an article written by Crescent Dragonwagon that appeared in the spring 1982 *ALAN Review* (published by the National Council of Teachers of English). In the article Dragonwagon told how Zindel had helped her write *To Take a Dare* and especially emphasized how understanding and generous he had been in working with her. What bothered Nilsen was Dragonwagon's filial relationship to Zindel's editor. She asked the question, "Would Dragonwagon have felt inspired to write this article if Zindel's reputation hadn't recently suffered from the lawsuit over the other less satisfactory partnership?" In effect, she believed that the piece's main purpose was to polish a tarnished reputation rather than to discuss the mechanics of a successful collaboration. Nilsen especially pointed an accusing finger at librarians, blaming them for often judging books on "personal feelings toward authors" and adopting "a charismatic approach to literary criticism." And she faulted them for expecting and encouraging young adult authors to write "self-promotional pieces," which, she complained, force good writers "to take time out from what they do best."[17]

So controversial was this segment of her talk that the official text of the speech published in *Top of the News* (issued by the Association for Library Service to Children and the Young Adult Services Division of the American Library Association) omitted the references to Zindel and Dragonwagon. The *School Library Journal* printed the missing excerpts in an editorial criticizing the "fan-club mentality" of teachers and librarians in their attitudes toward authors.[18]

As a novelist, Zindel was not content to write only for teenagers. In 1974, he published a picture book for children called *I Love My Mother,* a story he dedicated to Beatrice, which was the first name of his own mother who had died a few years before.[19] Narrated by a lonely child, it portrays the boy's love for his larger-than-life single-parent mother, who loves, protects, and understands him under trying circumstances. She teaches her son football and judo; she listens patiently to his tall tales; she buys him presents; she kisses him good night and protects him from the demons of his nightmares; and she shelters him from her poverty and loneliness. She is, in short, what a small boy imagines a perfect mother to be.

One of the primary attractions of *I Love My Mother* is the colorful, realistic pictures drawn by John Melo. The *School Library Journal* praised the book as "an uncommon and most successful blending of picture and text."[20] The review in the *Bulletin of the Center for Children's Books,* however, perceptively pointed out that "there was nothing in the text to prepare a child for the poignant hopelessness of the last pages," where the boy expresses his deep loneliness because he cannot visit his father.[21] The reason this book might be considered too adult for young children is that Zindel was writing the story as much for himself "to make up for the past" as he was writing for children. "There is a need in everyone," he comments, "to want to give wonderful things to your mother."[22] This fantasized slice of his childhood is Zindel's retrospective gift to his own mother, even though he had mixed feelings about her.

But "mixed feelings" is too positive a description for how Zindel feels about *When a Darkness Falls,* his only venture into adult fiction. For years, he had thought about writing a best-seller and believed he could trade on the popularity of *The Exorcist,* which made clear the public's seemingly insatiable capacity for being shocked. While he was living in California in the early eighties, Zindel saw his darkest nightmares and bloodiest horror story ideas spill over into reality, with almost daily newspaper headlines about the "freeway killer" and similar sensations. If he could invest a novel with enough shock and gore, he thought, it could become the best-seller he hoped for.

When a Darkness Falls tries to be a suspenseful murder mystery about Detective Leichteiman's attempts to solve a series of grisly murders of young women in Hollywood.[23] Against this backdrop, Zindel develops the characters of screenwriter Jack Krenner and his novelist wife, Marjorie, and traces their ensnarement in the frenetic Hollywood life-style of material wealth and spiritual angst. It soon becomes apparent to the reader that there is a horrible link between Krenner's disintegrating cocaine-ridden life and the murders of the young women. There is probably also a small kernel of Zindel's own experience in Hollywood—albeit highly exaggerated and fictionalized. (Jack and Marjorie Krenner have two children the same age as the Zindels' children at that time.) In a review characteristic of the reaction to the book, *Library Journal* critic Ann Fisher said the novel was "a grisly page-turner" filled with "psychological clichés and two-dimensional characters . . . and [the] sex-and-violence the plot seems to demand."[24]

Zindel agrees with this harsh assessment. He puts the blame on his failure to plot carefully and on his too calculating effort to write a best-seller. Nevertheless, many who read the book were pulled into the horror and were frightened by it, including his own wife who read the novel alone at night in an empty house. But Zindel says the book was "a big mistake. If I could make it disappear," he adds, "I would do it."[25]

4. Women in Distress: The Plays of Paul Zindel

Just after Zindel was released from the tuberculosis sanatorium where he had spent eighteen months recuperating from the disease, the seventeen-year-old high school senior submitted a play to a contest sponsored by the American Cancer Society. He won a silver ballpoint pen as a prize, and ever since, he has been interested in creating drama. Many Americans, in fact, know him not as the author of young adult novels but as the Pulitzer Prize–winning playwright of *The Effect Of Gamma Rays on Man-in-the-Moon Marigolds*. Zindel himself believes that his major literary talent and interests lie in writing for the stage.[1]

Examining his plays in the context of his young adult novels shows both some striking similarities to his stories for teenagers and some revealing differences. Unlike his novels, the plays were written for an adult audience, and they contain mostly adult characters. (One exception is *Gamma Rays*'s portrayal of teenagers Tillie and Ruth, whose characterizations ultimately led to Harper & Row's invitation to Zindel to write young adult novels.) Whereas the young adult stories depict troubled adolescents resolving their problems, Zindel's plays are mostly about neurotic women who are unable to overcome their crippling obsessions and depressions. These women in distress bear a close resemblance to the neurotic mothers of the author's young adult novels.

Zindel's dramatic characterizations have been influenced by Tennessee Williams's plays about fragile and loveless women.[2] Like Williams, Zindel seems to believe that the vulnerability inherent in his female characters can lead to the development of sensitivity and imagination. The teenage heroines in his young adult novels—such as Edna in *Pardon Me* and Lorraine in the two *Pigman* books—clearly demonstrate this. But whereas readers of Williams's plays feel pity and regret for his emotionally battered tragic women, readers of Zindel's plays are likely to feel contempt for his exaggerated female characters. Williams's characters are truly tragic because they are not equal to the world's demands; Zindel's women appear to be perversely crazy, destroying the lives of those around them as well as their own.

Zindel has written six published plays, three unpublished plays, and several teleplays and screenplays. *Dimensions of Peacocks,* about a visiting nurse and her confused son, was written under the tutelage of Edward Albee while Zindel was at Wagner College, and it was performed in New York City in 1959. Two other plays— *Euthanasia and the Endless Hearts* and *A Dream of Swallows*— were written and performed in New York during Zindel's first years as a high school teacher in the early 1960s. None of the three plays was critically well received, and all closed soon after their initial performances.

Zindel was not taken seriously as a playwright until he wrote *The Effect of Gamma Rays on Man-in-the-Moon Marigolds* in 1963. But success did not come immediately. *Gamma Rays* first played in Houston for six weeks in 1965. It took five years and many revisions before it was produced in New York and won the 1971 Pulitzer Prize.

The Effect of Gamma Rays on Man-in-the-Moon Marigolds has to be one of the strangest titles ever given to a play. Zindel got the idea for it from one of his high school students who responded to an ad in a comic book for marigold seeds exposed to gamma rays.[3] Clive Barnes of the *New York Times* thought it was "one of the most discouraging titles yet devised by man."[4] Discouraging or not, the eccentricity of the title prepares the reader to expect the unusual. A bitter and cynical Beatrice Hunsdorfer lives with her teenage daughters, Ruth and Tillie.[5] Her entire income is derived from her caring for Nanny, an elderly deaf mute abandoned by her daughter. Both Tillie and Ruth, although conditioned by Beatrice to be dependent on her and to accept her frequent outbursts of frustration and anger, struggle to forge an identity for themselves. Ruth, however, is directionless and easily intimidated; she very often is overcome with seizures brought on by her mother's verbal abuse. (Zindel remembers that when his older sister, Betty, was twelve years old, she had chronic convulsions.)[6] Ruth's only interest is a rabbit given to her sister by a high school science teacher—a pet that Beatrice repeatedly threatens to kill. But Tillie, although shy and withdrawn, clings to the rabbit and concentrates her energies on a science project involving marigold seeds exposed to radiation. The results of her experiment show that some seeds die, some live on normally, and others survive in a mutated state (with double flowers and enlarged stems, for example). Tillie is happily surprised when her project wins a competition.

Beatrice, however, cannot bear either Tillie's success or her own failures. She kills Tillie's rabbit and then bitterly tells her daughter, "I hate the world" (p. 107). Ruth fares no better; she succumbs to a seizure after learning of the slaughter of the one thing she loved. But Tillie is redeemed by her success. "My experiment," she exclaims in exultation, "has made me feel important—every atom in me, in everybody, has come from the sun—from places beyond our dreams" (p. 109).

By ending with Tillie's affirmation of life, Zindel tells his readers and himself that it is possible not only to survive but also to overcome maternal "toxic radiation." This is a theme Zindel has dealt with over and over again in his novels for teenagers. He projects on Tillie—as he does on Maggie, Lauri, and Edna—many traits he had as a teenager (shyness, vulnerability, resolve, curiosity, quest for self-identity) and pits her against a mother who seems to be a combination of Marsh's drunken, schizoid mother and Chris's overbearing mother. Beatrice Hunsdorfer is called "Betty the Loon" early in the play, and although alcohol was not a problem for Zindel's own mother (whose name, it will be recalled, was also Beatrice), the author admits that Tillie and Ruth's mother is his own parent "in nightmarish exaggeration."[7]

Another similarity between Zindel's young adult novels and this play is the cosmic resolution of the worldly conflicts in each work. Tillie's exultant exclamation recalls the conclusion of *Pardon Me:* "At last there were the stars set in their place" (p. 262). Chris ends *Confessions of a Teenage Baboon* with a comparable statement: "I began to look past the moon, past all the great satellites of Jupiter, and dream upon the stars" (p. 154). Even in Zindel's adult novel, *When a Darkness Falls,* he reaches for the cosmic in the aftermath of the devastating tragedy depicted in the novel and says that Marjorie Krenner, the wife of Jack Krenner, the pathological killer who has just been shot to death by the police, "would look beyond to the distant horizon, to the first signs that soon dawn would be there" (p. 243). In the play and the novels, Zindel uses science—represented by the physical order of the universe—as a metaphor for security and hope, and as a source of meaning and comfort for his unhappy characters. "I remember thinking," Zindel told a *Time* interviewer after winning the Pulitzer Prize, "that all carbon atoms on earth had to come from the sun. The idea of being linked to the universe by these atoms, which really don't die, gave me a feeling of meaning."[8]

There is, however, very little meaning (or comfort, for that matter) in the confused and empty female lives dramatized in Zindel's short play *The Ladies Should Be in Bed,* a teleplay commissioned by National Educational Television after the author's successful NET production of *Gamma Rays.* It is based on Zindel's remembrance of the time when he was living in the Staten Island castle that inspired *The Pigman.* Next to the castle was a brightly lit large brick house with picture windows. Every week at an appointed time, he would see four women playing bridge at a table visible through the window. They also saw him watching them. What, Zindel kept thinking, were *they* thinking about him?[9]

In the play, the four card-playing women gossip about others and berate and mock one another, all the while focusing their attention on a young man in an adjacent house that was formerly a convent.[10] The man they gawk at stands naked in the window staring out at the trees and sky. In speculating about what is going on in the house, the four reveal their personalities and express their sexual attitudes, which run the gamut from repression to ostentation. At four o'clock every day, they notice that two boys and a girl meet with this mysterious exhibitionist. So involved are these women in their sexual neuroses that when one of them resolves to call the father of one of the boys and the mother of the girl to accuse their neighbor of endangering the morals of their children, the other three acquiesce in this malicious prank and wait expectantly for the inevitable showdown (which never takes place). In the meantime, the four continue their abusive banter, until the aged and infirm mother of the hostess makes her way to the top of the stairs and shouts down to them: "Ladies should be in bed. The ladies should be in bed" (p. 55).

The life image of the young man in this play derived from Zindel's experience at the castle and his source for Lloyd Dipardi in *Confessions of a Teenage Baboon*—a character who befriended teenagers and raised dark suspicions among residents of the community.[11] NET had commissioned the play but considered it "too ugly for television" and refused to air it, according to Zindel.[12] In its stead, he submitted another teleplay he had written called *Let Me Hear You Whisper*.[13] This is a short, didactic drama inspired by Zindel's reading on dolphin research. The play shows that he is as suspicious of the human use of science as he is trusting of the physical order of the universe. Portrayed in this touching drama is a commodity often missing from the lives of Zindel's adult literary characters—love. Here the love is between Helen, a science lab cleaning woman, and a dolphin about to be killed because the mammal will not cooperate in an experiment being conducted for military development. When Helen discovers the reason the scientists are trying to get the dolphin to communicate, she first tries to rescue the mammal. But the experimenters catch her in the act and fire her. Just at this point, the dolphin bleeps out the word L-O-V-E. Surprised and excited by this turn of events, the scientists try to convince Helen to stay on the job and work with them. Helen, however, wants no part of it and leaves. How much good this does the dolphin or how much it sets back the military experiment is unclear. But Zindel does succeed in casting a dark shadow on scientific experimentation—the same goal he had when in *Gamma Rays* he satirically depicted one of Tillie's competitors boiling a live cat and skinning it in order to understand the anatomy of the animal.

Zindel returns to his forsaken female characters in his second full-length play, *And Miss Reardon Drinks a Little*. "There is less unity here than in *Gamma Rays*," the author says of *Miss Reardon*, "but there is better, more dynamic writing."[14] Although some critics disagreed with this self-appraisal, the play is probably Zindel's most biting, dramatic, and emotional portrayal of out-of-control women. Originally written as a one-act play in 1966, *Miss Reardon* was revised and enlarged several times before its New York performance in 1971.

The play concerns the three Reardon sisters—Ceil, Catherine, and Anna—each professionally involved in education.[15] Their mother, who has died seven months before, left them with psychological scars. She made them suspicious and afraid of males—like Lorraine's mother in *The Pigman*. She bullied and dominated them until they had little self-esteem—like Chris's mother in *Confessions*. And her neurotic behavior warped their lives as Lloyd's eccentric and destructive mother warped his. Like Nanny, who was abandoned by her daughter in *Gamma Rays*, the Reardons' mother had been left to die alone by Catherine and Ceil. Only Anna had helped her, and now Anna is suffering a nervous breakdown from the emotional strain of watching her die. In addition, Anna has been recently suspended from her high school teaching job after trying to seduce one of her students. Throughout the play, she is pictured as hopelessly paranoic and dependent on Catherine for almost everything. A teacher at the same school as Anna, Catherine is a sharp-tongued alcoholic, deeply hurt by Ceil years before when her sister stole Catherine's only boyfriend. Ceil, a sweet-talking and two-faced school administrator, appears to be the only "success" in the family, but her veneer of respectability is shattered quickly by Catherine's pointed accusations.

A motley collection of recriminations tossed around by Catherine and Ceil (as well as by two irascible neighbors), the play ends in family disintegration. A guilty and deflated Ceil angrily walks out, Anna screams "I'm losing my mind," and Catherine tells Anna that "everyone's going crazy" (p. 43). In a token attempt at reconciliation, Catherine reaches out and touches Anna consolingly, but this seems little more than a gesture in the face of all the broken lives on and off the stage. The maternal toxic fallout in this play has left only mutated survivors.

Perhaps written as a comic antidote to the histrionics of *Miss Reardon,* Zindel's third full-length play, *The Secret Affairs of Mildred Wild,* is billed as a "comedy in three acts," but it reads more like a farce gone sour.[16] Mildred Wild is a frustrated, alienated woman who lives with her diabetic husband, Roy, in the back of their small New York City candy store, from which they barely eke out a living. Roy's sister, Helen, pays the rent. Roy wears a wig to cover his bare skull (and empty head) and gorges on so much candy he is in a semicomatose state at one point. He is having an affair with their landlady, Bertha Gale. Mildred hides from reality by making herself up heavily and fantasizing in the style of Walter Mitty about classic films like *King Kong* and *Gone with the Wind.* When Mildred wins a potpourri of prizes on a television game show, her biggest dream seems to have come true: she is to be given a Hollywood screen test. But she soon finds that the screen test and most of the other prizes are as empty as the fantasy she has made of her life. Although disillusioned and defeated, Mildred and Roy at the end of the play come to their senses. He gives up his wig and she her cosmetics, thereby cutting the ties to their make-believe worlds. They decide to accept Helen's proposal that they take care of a vacant convent in return for being allowed to live there rent-free.

Like *Miss Reardon, Mildred Wild* abounds with insults exchanged among Mildred, Roy, and Helen, but the harshness of the barbs is offset by sight gags and more humor than appears in the earlier play. But despite the fact that Mildred and Roy come to terms with each other at the end of the play, Mildred is not much better off than the three hapless Reardon sisters.

Ladies at the Alamo, Zindel's most recent play, was performed in New York City in 1975. Probably the strongest female character in any of Zindel's plays appears here in the person of Dede Cooper, "a gutsy, honest and striking" Texas woman who is the director of a newly built lavish theater complex.[17] Many have speculated that the source of this character is Nina Vance, the director of the Alley Theatre in Houston, where Zindel was playwright-in-residence in 1967.[18] But the author denies it, claiming that Nina Vance is "a refined, strong lady," whereas Dede is "a gruff, down-to-earth fighter."[19]

Dede has just come from her mother's funeral, and she is immediately thrust into a power struggle with her benefactor, Joanne, who claims that under Dede's management the theater is losing money. Although threatening to fire her, Joanne instead brings in Dede's old nemesis to help run the company—a woman named Shirley who was once an Academy Award nominee and is now recovering from a nervous breakdown. The theater troupe that Dede directs includes a loud-mouthed, theatrical, and alcoholic actress named Bella and an ineffectual and overweight actress named Beatrice (again!), whose nickname is "Suits" because she wears pantsuits. With the help of her friend Bella, Dede fights back and undermines Shirley's credibility by proving she is a sexual eccentric and a lesbian. She then verbally browbeats Joanne into submission, emerging a clear victor.

Confronted with a conspiracy to embarrass her for the way she runs the theater, Dede relies on her strong instinct for survival, digging up dirt on her adversaries to take attention away from her own mistakes. Nevertheless, she is preoccupied as the play ends not with the fruits of victory but with guilt-ridden memories of her mother—which connects her to the Zindel lineage of female characters. And the other women in the play reflect the Hunsdorfer-Reardon pattern: alcoholic, hypocritical, schizophrenic, sexually repressed, and bizarre.

Not only do Zindel's female dramatic personalities resemble many of the parental authority figures in his young adult novels; they also repeat some unusual behavior. Mildred Wild's sister-in-law, Helen, for instance, compulsively steals from the sanatorium in which she works, and Fleur Stein—the Reardons' odd neighbor—steals sugar, salt, and paper napkins from the teachers' lunchroom. Such work-related petty thievery is also the hallmark of the decadence of many of Zindel's female characters in his stories for teenagers (for example, Yvette in *I Never Loved Your Mind* and Chris's mother, Helen, in *Confessions of a Teenage Baboon*). Similarly, Fleur Stein and Chris's mother both manifest a strange reluctance to use bathrooms in homes other than their own and have a propensity for urinating in milk bottles—an eccentricity that plays an important role in Zindel's *When a Darkness Falls*.

The author also employs some of the same literary devices in his plays that he has used in his young adult novels. For example, he names characters to reflect their role in the play. Beatrice Hunsdorfer is a contemporary Hun in her domineering control over her daughters. Mildred Wild is always fantasizing and seldom grounded in reality. Mr. Fridge is a coldhearted assistant to the scientist, Dr. Crocus, who acts like a morally lower form of life than the dolphin he is exploiting in *Let Me Hear You Whisper*.

Zindel's plays exaggerate and embellish the themes, styles, and characters that appear in his young adult novels. Why this is so probably can be traced to Zindel's own observation that the main difference between his plays and his novels is his audience.[20] When he writes for teenagers, he is adhering to a set of guidelines; he is teaching and learning lessons, and he is more controlled in his writing. His main goal is to keep teenage readers turning the pages. Zindel seems to have less control in his plays, relying on sharp-sounding insults and argumentative banter as a substitute for communication between his characters and using melodrama to resolve conflicts. The problem-solving teenagers of *The Pigman* and *Pardon Me* almost never come on stage in his plays. Instead, Zindel spotlights the adults who cause the problems for these enterprising teenagers, but they are drawn in "nightmarish exaggeration" and they seldom end up as better people. These irredeemable and forsaken adults do not seem capable of absorbing the lessons of life that Zindel's adolescent heroes and heroines— and the author himself—have learned in his young adult novels.

5. How I Write and Who I Am: The Subconscious and the Conscious

For Paul Zindel, the creative process of writing rests heavily on planning and structure. But the catalyst that sets this process into motion is his subconscious, which digests and processes facts and filters them through his consciousness. "Writing is primarily daydreaming," Zindel says, "and good writing is daydreaming with a technical basis."[1] Without careful and detailed planning, the writer lacks the ordering elements that distinguish the mediocre from the superior; without daydreams, however, the writer lacks the creative energy that fuels the entire process.

Daydreaming is not just idle reverie. Because Zindel has trouble remembering facts, he often repeats them to himself just before he goes to sleep the night before he plans to write. Then he lets his subconscious process the facts with dreams; he calls this a form of "spiritual refueling."[2] When he awakes the next morning, he is ready to write.

Zindel's editor, Charlotte Zolotow, has noted that he does not work as methodically or as compulsively as many other prolific writers do. She says that Hemingway, for example, wrote for four hours every morning and then stopped promptly at the end of this period—even leaving sentences uncompleted if his time was up.[3]

Zindel, with characteristic self-deprecation and exaggeration, calls his writing routine "sheer laziness." He usually writes in the morning for two hours at a stretch, but, he confesses, "I don't force myself at all. I actually wait until the material is ready to come out."[4] He says that the most successful works he has written are those that were "written without conscious awareness"—such as *The Pigman* and *Gamma Rays.*[5]

Zindel does put a considerable amount of research into his young adult novels, however. For example, before writing *The Girl Who Wanted a Boy,* he visited several video arcades and other teen hangouts in southern California to get the details right. And while he contemplated how to prepare the climactic scene of *Pardon Me,* he bought and launched a firecracker which exploded eight hundred feet in the air in the shape of an American flag. Zindel acknowledges that the kind of empirical research he does forces him to keep up with the trends and fads of the popular youth culture and that this is one of the reasons he likes to write novels for teenagers.[6]

Of course, the writing process is not just daydreaming and dabbling in teenage recreations. Before writing a word, Zindel carefully plans and structures the novel in longhand and then usually refines this initial planning draft into a rough typewritten form without bothering about correct spelling or punctuation. (He does not use a word processor because the screen hurts his eyes after protracted use.) His next step is to go through his plan chapter by chapter and daydream about what he wants to write, penciling ideas in with arrows. Then he types a first draft and again jots in changes. This revised version he sends to a professional typist who produces a clean copy.[7]

At this point, Zindel's publisher begins editorial revisions. When the author first began writing young adult novels, he left the proofreading to others, thinking that his job was done when he handed in his revised draft. But he now realizes that proofreading is an integral part of the entire writing process and that he has to be involved in this if he is going to assume responsibility for the final manuscript.[8] Once the novel is published, Zindel tries to leave it and go on to something else. Until recently, in fact, he did not even reread his young adult novels after they were published.

The texts of Zindel's stories for teenagers reveal his interest in character development, dialogue, and plot action, but very little concern for physical description. That Zindel is color-blind may be a reason for this: he can distinguish only black and brown clearly. Years ago, when he showed his friend, actress Maureen Stapleton, his Staten Island bachelor apartment, she commented—to his amazement—that she had never seen such a brown apartment.[9]

It is not surprising, then, that Zindel has for a long time found himself out of step with clothing styles. But he cannot blame his color blindness entirely for this, even though he used to wear only black and brown suits. Zindel's indifference to what he wore and how he looked probably had more to do with his dissatisfaction with his physical appearance. After winning the Pulitzer Prize in 1971, he did make a concerted effort to read *GQ* for help in this department. But he never seemed to get it right. "By the time I knew how my hair should be combed," he says, "it fell out; by the time I knew how I should dress, I got fat." Despite these disclaimers, however, Zindel at fifty-one is neither completely bald nor unduly obese, although his six–foot frame does have less hair on top and more excess weight than ten years ago. He started wearing a beard when his hair began thinning, but he has since learned from reading *GQ* that one should wear a beard not only to compensate for loss of hair but also if one has a disproportionately small chin—which he does. Occasionally, Zindel has experimented with shaving off his beard, but he now feels he needs it.[10]

Turning fifty spurred him to evaluate his career and artistic aspirations, and his eclectic reading has lately focused on ways to establish personal life goals. One of the few areas Zindel does not explore much in his reading is politics. When artists venture into the political arena, he thinks, they are often out of their league, and "the type of hysteria" that results furthers neither politics nor art. Although he describes himself as apolitical, he expresses a sensitivity to social injustice and a sympathy for those who are victims of discrimination. But his approach is nonideological, and his involvement is limited to his literary art.[11]

"Nonideological" is also a fair description of Zindel's religious beliefs. In childhood, he was exposed to watered-down versions of both Catholicism and Protestantism, but neither satisfied his spiritual needs. During the sixties, his acquaintances discovered Eastern religions when they were a major ingredient of the youth subculture, but he was never able to accept their other-worldly focus. It is inaccurate, however, to describe him as an agnostic because he sees a need for a belief in a deity. "I wish there *were* a God," he says. Whether he believes in a God, Zindel lightheartedly explains, depends "a lot on how miserably my life is going."[12] This facetiousness, however, belies the spiritual quality Zindel has shown most clearly in his young adult novel *Harry and Hortense at Hormone High,* in which he examined how out of touch we all are with our human roots.

One of the ways he has reestablished his own roots is through his family. He is very close to his wife, Bonnie, a former scriptwriter and public relations specialist, and he has been instrumental in encouraging her to write for teenagers. And David and Lizabeth, the Zindels' children, are his joy. He remembers their births as clearly as he recalls anything in his life. Until the time David was born, Zindel says, he had been able to find emotional catharsis only through his writing. But in the delivery room, a barrier was broken, and he remembers crying from happiness and excitement for the first time in his life.[13]

When Zindel is asked how he spends his spare time, his two children figure prominently in his response. He relishes his time with them. He helps them with their school lessons and marvels at their capacity for learning and their spontaneous creativity. He takes David to Mets baseball games and bicycles through Manhattan's crowded streets with his daughter. And thirteen-year-old David and eleven-year-old Liza are now at an age, Zindel says with excitement, when he can use their experiences in his young adult novels, something he is already planning for his next one.[14]

6. The Game of Life

"This book is not pornography," a reviewer of *Pardon Me, You're Stepping on My Eyeball* generously conceded, "but neither does it have any redeeming features."[1] That sums up the feelings of many parents, teachers, librarians, and critics about the young adult novels of Paul Zindel—with the exception of *The Pigman*. Authors of stories for teenagers are often criticized for being too sexually explicit (as are Norma Klein and Judy Blume) or too willing to indulge in four-letter words (as is Kin Platt). Zindel, however, can't be faulted for these reasons. Although he has dealt with sexual relationships in many of his novels, he has never written sexually explicit scenes in these stories. He either makes indirect references to sexual activity or has the action take place offstage. Nor has his language been a problem. When John Conlan in the two *Pigman* books wants to swear, for example, Zindel gives his hero the cautious good sense of the politician: John devises typewriter codes such as @#$% that mask the cursing.

What upsets the critics about Zindel's works are his attitudes toward life, which many adults find cynical and offensive and certainly not worthy of being passed on to the leaders of our next generation. They oppose his characterization of parents and school personnel as one-dimensional imbeciles, and they resent his seeming glorification of youth. They regard his emphasis on death, loneliness, alcoholism, broken families, and sickness as a statement on the futility of life, and they think he thereby justifies the creation of teenage heroes who thrive on their rebellion against authority. In short, they see Zindel as a panderer and a corrupter rather than an enlightener of youth.

So strong are these sentiments that many don't go beyond their gut reaction to Zindel's stories. With righteous indignation, they parrot the tone and substance of one critic's summary of *Pardon Me:* "Other kids are criminoid or kooks. Parents are psychotic pains. Teachers are at least half-tetched. The government is grimy. All realities are wretched."[2] Broadsides like this grossly overstate two weaknesses of Zindel's novels—character stereotyping and plot repetitiveness. They also completely misrepresent Zindel's picture of reality.

The irony of the complaints is that Zindel's values are as pure and positive as the views of those who point an accusing finger at him. All realities are *not* wretched in Zindel's stories. The teenage protagonists, almost all of whom begin as lonely and confused adolescents, work hard at overcoming obstacles of matter and spirit to become more caring, communicative, and wise people at the story's conclusion. "I tell [readers]," Zindel says, "that tomorrow becomes today through self-inspection and action and belief, that their minds come equipped by God or Nature with the spirit and means to be joyful and intimate with their fellow human beings."[3] He has also written, "Love and trust seem to be at the bottom of every element in the great mystery of life that we are all trying to solve."[4] These statements indicate the creed of a believer in life, not a cynic.

In *The Pigman's Legacy,* the sequel to Zindel's first novel, the colonel teaches a game to John and Lorraine—the game of life (p. 59). It is a kind of Rorschach test in which the way a player interprets various constants shows how he or she views important aspects of life. Although the game is transparently didactic, it serves as a good value model for all of Zindel's young adult novels; it also highlights what the author thinks is important and what he is trying to communicate to his readers.

To begin the game, close your eyes and imagine yourself walking down a road. This is "the road of life," and how you describe it signifies the direction, certainty, and overall happiness of your life. You see a key lying in the road, which represents "the key of knowledge"; the way you describe it indicates how you view school and learning (which, as John points out in the story, are two very different things). Then you see a cup lying in the middle of the road; this is "the cup of love" and what you say about the way it looks reveals your view of love. (If the cup is dirty but worth cleaning, for example, your attitude toward love can be changed.) Next, you come to a tree alongside the road, which symbolizes your sex life; your description of the tree shows how satisfied you are in this aspect of your life. (John, for example, says that the tree is big and filled with shamrocks and that it has many twisting roots and leaves. The colonel interprets this to mean that John's sex life will be "rich and full.") Finally, you come to a wall "as thick as eternity and as high as eternity." That is "the wall of death," and what you do with it signifies how you will deal with the threat of death (p. 68).

The underlying assumption of this game is freedom of will. No matter how bad the circumstances of one's life—and Zindel's imagination conjures up some rock-bottom examples—no matter how alienated one is from human contact, by opening up to life's experiences one can transform oneself into a feeling, loving, and responsible human being.

How does one become this paragon of humanity? Zindel believes strongly in the precepts embodied in the ancient and now famous statement of Hillel the Elder: "If I am not for myself, who will be for me? If I am only for myself, what am I? And if not now, when?"[5] Before claiming to do good for others, one must learn to assume responsibility for one's own actions. And before being able to be aware of the consequences of one's actions, one must learn to accept and respect oneself.

For Zindel, being a good person is a process that begins with "examining self-hate and feelings of inadequacy and act[ing] to stop the process." He believes that teenagers must put a high premium on "taking care of themselves" and even being "selfish if they must" so that "their souls stay intact and their hearts never die."[6] One can't be a responsible and loving person before coming to terms with oneself and one's own interests.

This was a hard-won truth for Zindel because, as a fatherless boy growing up on Staten Island, he felt lonely and alienated. "I felt worthless as a child," he reflects, "and dared to speak and act out my true feelings only in fantasy and secret."[7] In almost every one of his young adult novels, Zindel's teenage heroes learn first how to respect themselves by coming out of the closet of "fantasy and secrecy" and expressing their true selves openly. Then—and only then—are they able to recognize the social and moral consequences of their actions and the fulfilling power of loving someone else.

A look at the principal teenage protagonists in three books—*The Pigman, The Pigman's Legacy,* and *Pardon Me, You're Stepping on My Eyeball*—illustrates vividly that Hillel's age-old wisdom is deeply embedded in Zindel's writings.

John and Lorraine of the *Pigman* novels are very different from each other, but they have one trait in common: they both lack self-esteem. Lorraine's divorced mother, sexually repressed and bitter after a bad marriage, constantly instills in her daughter the view that all men want from women is sex. She tries to cripple any sexual feelings and feminine identity that Lorraine might still possess by daily ridiculing her daughter's appearance and by setting unreasonable limits on her friendship with John. It is no wonder that Lorraine is self-conscious and even paranoic: "I've got to admit that when anyone looks at me, I'm sure they're noticing how awful my hair is or I'm too fat or my dress is funny" (p. 15).

John also harbors feelings of inadequacy brought on by an overbearing, alcoholic father and a compulsive, repressed mother. His mother's abhorrence of touching makes it difficult for John to express his emotions openly. When he was three, she threatened to "slice" his penis up "like pepperoni" after she caught him touching that "sensuous part" of his body (p. 112). As if this was not enough to create a stillborn soul, his father—when he's not drunk—seems to devote a major portion of his energies to the control of John's activities. For example, when his father wants John to stop talking with Lorraine on the phone, he puts a lock on the instrument. Unlike Lorraine, who is unable to express anger, John rebels against his father's punitive childishness by going him one step further: he puts airplane glue in the keyhole of the lock, "so no one could use the phone" (p. 21). John's explanation is that he goes "a little crazy" when he is "being picked on or not being trusted" (p. 21). It is this lack of parental respect which causes him to write graffiti like "A rotten science teacher has given me a drug to change into a teeny-weeny mosquito." In this bit of street wisdom, John at once is expressing anger at his parents (transferred to the school) and exhibiting his own low self-esteem. Both the antagonism between John and his father and his poor self-image lead him to drink compulsively—self-destructive behavior that emulates that of his father.

The lack of trust John and Lorraine receive from their parents explains why they so easily become friends with Mr. Pignati. The friendship they share with the Pigman also brings the two teenagers closer together. In a memorable scene, John and Lorraine discover the Pigman's bedroom while exploring the house, and Lorraine dresses up in the clothes of the Pigman's dead wife, pretending to play a romantic scene with John. Their make-believe script calls for them to kiss, but John suddenly finds the fantasy "very real": "When I moved my lips away from hers," he says, "we just looked at each other and somehow we were not acting anymore." Scared by what she has felt and still under the influence of her mother, Lorraine blurts out, "I think we'd better go downstairs" (p. 134). This is the first mutual realization that their friendship is blossoming into something more.

Just as Lorraine can't undo years of submissiveness to her mother and a long-standing inferiority complex, John can't throw off his long-simmering anger against his parents and eliminate the scars of this relationship. His addiction to alcohol leads to an orgiastic party at the Pigman's house, resulting in its destruction and ultimately in the death of the Pigman. As John stands over the dead body of Mr. Pignati, he admits what Lorraine has been telling him—that his drinking is an expression of self-hate. Once he can admit that, he can assume responsibility for all that he has done. Taking Lorraine's hand, he reflects on the tragic events: "We had trespassed—been where we didn't belong and we were being punished for it. Mr. Pignati had paid with his life. But when he died, something in us had died as well. There was no one else to blame anymore. . . . And there was no place to hide" (p. 182). It would seem that John and Lorraine have learned their lesson.

This, however, is something easier said than done. A year and a half later, John and Lorraine are still torn with guilt about the Pigman, but they both view the episode as a rite of passage from childhood. At the outset of *The Pigman's Legacy,* John says: "If you've never felt guilty about anything, then you must be a lily-white angel from heaven" (p. 6). Lorraine makes the point even more forcefully: "The Pigman killed our childhood. . . . the day your childhood dies is probably the first day you really know what guilt is" (pp. 8–9).

These concerns are at the forefront of their minds when the two first meet the colonel in the Pigman's house. John's first thought is that they are being drawn into the colonel's life "by Fate, just to punish us." The colonel, John says, is "a reminder of all the things we've done wrong" (p. 39). Lorraine correctly sees this as John's guilt, but she too takes the view that the event has been put there for a purpose: she sees it as an opportunity for them, "a second chance" (p. 40).

As they become more enmeshed in the colonel's life, this second chance to make good with the Pigman becomes a first chance for John and Lorraine to express their feelings for each other. In a secret paragraph (which she hides from John), Lorraine writes that her involvement in the Pigman tragedy has freed her from an emotonal straitjacket: "If knowing the Pigman did anything for me, it at least taught me that kids are responsible for their own lives at a certain age. And that's exactly why I'm now able to admit to myself that I love John Conlan very, very much, and even though he doesn't know it, I'm going to do everything in my power to make him my own" (p. 66). These are indeed strong words from a girl who when she first met John "was so embarrassed that [she] wanted to cry because [she] thought he was laughing" at her (p. 111).

John's secret paragraph comes later and independently of Lorraine's. In it, he admits to emotional deprivation and repression which he blames on his mother, and he devotes most of his paragraph to similar complaints. Only at the end does he talk about what is on his mind: "What I'm really trying to say is that . . . I was beginning to think how nice it would be to be able to put my arms around Lorraine and start kissing her" (p. 112). John too has come a long way from his "family of untouchables" (p. 112). He has begun to feel emotion toward someone else and to express it almost openly.

Lorraine soon has an opportunity to come out from behind her secret paragraph and openly express her love to John. When he compulsively gambles away the money the colonel has won in his Atlantic City frolic, John is shattered—not only by his irresponsible behavior but also by his recognition of his own destructiveness. Lorraine tries to help him by putting her arms around his neck and kissing him. "I could tell," she says, "he felt, at least for a moment, that he had some worth. . . . I needed him to know that I loved him fully, totally, desperately—and that I not only forgave him, but would stay with him until the end of the universe and the death of infinity" (p. 167).

As John and Lorraine leave the hospital after the colonel's death, John responds to Lorraine's declaration of devotion less poetically, but just as openly. "I want to spend my life with you," he tells her. Lorraine adds, "Our bodies were touching and there was no shame, there was no fear, there was no death" (p. 183).

Just as Lorraine reaches out to John in his lowest moments, the two teenagers have helped the colonel when he was most alone and in his greatest despair. Dolly, the colonel's friend, tells a guilty John and Lorraine that John's act of irresponsibility is not as important to the colonel as the love they have given him. "He loves you," she says to them, "because you saved him from being alone in his last days" (p. 170).

Zindel paints an even starker picture of two teenage misfits in

Pardon Me, You're Stepping on My Eyeball. Made to believe by her pushy, although well-intentioned, parents that she is a hopeless social recluse who can't attract boys, Edna Shinglebox thinks of herself as a "self-made yo-yo" (p. 6). Her mother complains, "What we want is for Edna to join the living. I never knew a fifteen-year-old who hadn't been out on a real date. . . . Girls hate her too" (p. 7). But Edna is so conditioned by her parents that she absolves them of any blame for her social backwardness.

"Marsh" Mellow is her classmate in their high school group therapy class, a ragged gathering of eccentric students and an even crazier psychologist-teacher. Unlike Edna's parents, Marsh's mother takes a direct approach in putting down her offspring. "You're a rotten, disgusting, revolting little son," she screeches at him. "I should have had an abortion" (p. 13). Rejected or at best ignored by this alcoholic mother, whom he calls "Schizoid Suzy," and unable to confront the fact of his father's death Marsh trusts no one and communicates only through boastful falsehoods. He lies about his father, whom he claims takes him on trips, and he lies about his relationships with girls. Every day he prays, "Oh, Lord, help my words to be gracious and tender today, for tomorrow I may have to eat them" (p. 15). Until he meets Edna, the only being he trusts is a small pet raccoon he carries in his shirt pocket. The animal is an orphan made parentless (as was Marsh) by a hit-and-run accident.

When they first meet in class, Edna is surprised that Marsh even speaks to her. Her second reaction is fear because he seems so strange: "He looked a little bit like the kind of person that would run around with a sign around his neck saying 'Support Mental Health or I'll kill you' " (p. 31). When Marsh, however, starts bragging about his father's exploits and his own special rating system for measuring the sexiness of females, Edna turns defensive and then becomes angry. When he asks her out, she retorts, "Thanks, but no thanks. I happen to rate boys alphabetically according to how much of a human being they are, and you're an 'X.' " She adds, "Besides, you talk about your father too much" (p. 35).

Why he does so is the problem, as Edna soon finds out. "Paranoid

Pete"—the name Marsh gives his father—is supposedly an unwilling inmate of a "nuthouse" where an amorphous "they" have him locked up. In letters purportedly sent to Marsh, Paranoid Pete outlines the devious plots of all his enemies. Marsh pleads with his new friend to read through the rambling letters and help him find and free his father.

Edna begins to suspect that Marsh himself has written the letters and is conning her in order to make her look foolish. She isn't able to confront Marsh with her suspicions, so she channels her anger toward her mother. For the first time, Edna tells her that parental interference has been "her main problem." Then she retires to her room and, looking in the mirror, talks to herself: "All Miss Edna Shinglebox ever did was keep her mouth shut and nod and be boring and try to agree with everybody. No more" (p. 118). On the heels of this enlightenment, Edna meets Marsh in the school cafeteria and calls him a liar face to face.

Next, she turns to her diary with a new self-confidence, and she records some disturbing dreams she has had. The most vivid ones deal with Marsh—and she resolves to untangle his problems because she now realizes that her own life is intertwined with his.

In an encounter with Schizoid Suzy, Edna learns the shocking truth about Marsh and his father: Paranoid Pete is dead, and Marsh keeps his cremated ashes in an urn under his bed along with a Fourth of July rocket set his father bought just before his fatal accident. The letters Marsh wrote, she discovers, were a desperate cry for help.

"I want to be a friend to this boy because I've never been a friend to anybody," she confesses to a fortune teller. "All I've been is selfish and interested in myself and so worried about myself." She writes to Marsh, who is still angry at her for calling him a liar: "I want to tell you my true feelings which is something I never did in my life. . . . I want us to be friends . . . and I need your friendship. If you want me to help you with your father, I will. I hurt inside when I think what you must be going through" (p. 189–90).

Marsh and Edna rush off with an urn full of ashes and the

rocket set to a fantasy mental hospital in Washington where Paranoid Pete is supposedly a prisoner. Marsh totals the car, and Edna pushes the urn off a nearby bridge. Remembering, however, that the fortune teller told her that Marsh needed to admit his father's death and engage in some symbolic, yet concrete act of purging, Edna decides to order Marsh to write down the one thing he hates most in the world. She promises to do the same, and scribbles, "I hate not being able to tell you I want to touch you." With hesitation and trembling, Marsh writes, "I hate that my father is dead" (pp. 260–61). He then lights the fuse of the rocket, and it blasts off, taking Marsh's problem with it. "Edna knew," the omniscient narrator of the story concludes, "as she watched the sky, that she was seeing the spectacular end of a ghost" (p. 262).

Although the fantastic events of the novel may stretch the limits of credulity, Edna's metamorphosis follows the pattern set out by Hillel: first, the establishment of self-confidence and then the reaching out to others in trust, responsibility, and love. It may be difficult to believe in Zindel's simplistic idea that with the purging of Marsh's ghost, all will be well with the boy and his relationship to Edna. "In an instant," Zindel's narrator ends the story, "there was the explosion of the last stage of the rocket, and then at last, there were the stars set in their proper place" (p. 262). Nevertheless, the process of healing has certainly begun for Marsh—and with the new and committed Edna hovering nearby, it is not hard to think that Marsh, like the stars, is well on his way to being "set in a proper place."

Being set in one's proper place is all-important to both Zindel and Hillel the Elder, and for both, the process for attaining this goal is the same. Through "self-inspection, action, and belief," Lorraine, John, Edna, and Marsh overcome a crippling past and establish self-esteem. From that point, they are able to reach out to others and "be intimate with their fellow human beings."[8] They have learned the truth: "If I am not for myself, who will be for me? If I am only for myself, what am I? If not now, when?"

7. Parents, Pedagogues, and Police

Paul Zindel on the one hand has been praised for creating strong, believable teenage characters and on the other has been criticized for his cardboard, mentally unstable adult caricatures. In most of Zindel's stories, it appears that he is humanizing his young adult protagonists while dehumanizing his adult authority figures, and this is no accident. Zindel, by design, focuses on fleshing out his teenage heroes. He does so because he believes adolescents want to read about their peers. For the same reason, he almost always tells the story from the viewpoint of the teenage characters.[1]

Zindel's adolescent heroes seem to define themselves not only by how they confront and resolve conflicts within themselves and among themselves, but also by how they relate to adults in authority. In portraying these adults, Zindel is trying not to create full characters but to provide challenges to his teenage protagonists, challenges that will eventually strengthen them.

"I'm minimizing the role of parents," Zindel says, "because [teenagers] get enough of them at home and [they] want them cast as small walk-ons."[2] Even a superficial reading of his novels, however, indicates that although the parents are not primary characters, they are far from "small walk-ons." In a less obvious but just as important way, the author's characterizations of teachers and police act not only as foils to the teenagers but also as representatives of social authority about which Zindel has strong opinions.

An examination of Zindel's attitudes toward parents, teachers, and police shows that he would like his teenage readers to be skeptical of this authority in their lives, but he would also like them to realize that outright rejection of authority makes social order impossible. The preponderance of villainous adult characters in his novels indicates that Zindel thinks his readers must confront the reality of imperfect adults, but not reject all of organized society. In fact, many of Zindel's protagonists are actually in search of the ideal parent, even while they express with sarcasm and hostility their disdain for the reality they encounter.

Of the three authority figures, parents play the most prominent role in Zindel's novels. John and Lorraine become involved in the Pigman's and the colonel's lives primarily because they are seeking a friendship with an adult to offset their unsatisfying relationships with their parents. In these two adults, the teenagers find people they can trust and who can trust them. Beverly Haley and Kenneth Donelson argue that John and Lorraine are seeking a parent substitute when they open themselves up to the lonely lives of the old men.[3] James Henke, however, says in a provocative essay that actually the two young adults are seeking to *be* parents; he believes that John and Lorraine treat Mr. Pignati and the colonel as if the two adults were *their* children.[4] Both possibilities are credible, and neither is mutually exclusive because John and Lorraine are looking for someone who will pay serious attention to them and someone they can love together as a couple. They are reacting to the empty place in their lives created by insensitive parents, and they seek the perfect parent and/or child. They want to be part of a family order they now lack.

My Darling, My Hamburger, a story ostensibly about how four teenagers react to sexual pressures in their lives, brings into clear focus Zindel's attitudes about the importance of family order and understanding parents. Maggie and Dennis act responsibly in a crisis, whereas Sean and Liz act selfishly and in confusion. The author is very definite about why the teenagers do what they do: Maggie's and Dennis's parents are loving, trusting, and supportive, and Sean's and Liz's are resentful, suspicious, and mercenary.

The connection between parental attitudes and their children's actions can be seen in the following episodes from the novel:

- Liz, upset at Sean's sexual pressure, decides to cancel her date with him and wants Maggie to cancel hers with Dennis. Maggie's mother notices she is not getting dressed for the dance, and Maggie explains that Liz had a fight with Sean and she has decided to stay home with her. "Oh," her mother says noncommittally. Maggie asks her mother what she thinks of Dennis. "He's cute . . . and he's respectful," she answers. After thanking her daughter for helping with the dishes, she asks Maggie if Dennis has kissed her yet. Blushing, Maggie admits that he has. "Good. He's supposed to," her mother says—and then compares Dennis's attributes to the virtues of Maggie's father. (p. 34)

- Dennis has just received a call from Maggie breaking his date. Confused and disappointed, he can't tell his parents the truth, so he tells them she will be a little late. "That was nice of her to call," remarks his mother. "This girl you're going out with," his father says, "you make sure you respect her, young man." (p. 40)

- After Sean has rescued Liz from a sexual attack by her date, they go driving in Sean's car and get stuck with a flat tire. Worried about what her suspicious parents will say if she gets home late, she calls them to let them know what has happened. "Get home here. Do you hear me, you little tramp?" her stepfather screams. She returns to Sean's car and says, "I'm not in a hurry to go home anymore." (p. 93)

- When Sean learns about Liz's pregnancy, he reluctantly asks advice from his father. But he attributes the problem to a friend. First, his father says, make sure there *is* a problem. "She might be saying it to get even with

him for something. . . . she might be pulling the whole
thing to make sure she catches a husband with a little
money," he tells Sean. Second, the boy should find out if
it's really his. "She may have been spreading it around,
if you know what I mean," he warns his son. Then the
boy should try to scare the girl. If that doesn't work, Sean
is advised, he should get her an abortion. "Suppose," Sean
counters, "he loves her." "Boy, your friend doesn't know
what love is," his father retorts. "Tell your friend to give
that girl a kick in the behind now and get it over with."
Finally, his father wonders aloud, "Why doesn't this boy
ask his own father?" Sean answers, "He can't talk to
him." (pp. 123–25)

Zindel strongly believes that parental authority should consist
of support, trust, and love. When these elements are missing or
are warped by values centered on money and power, teenagers
lack guidance and may engage in self-destructive actions.

Another aspect of positive parenthood, according to Zindel, is
that fathers and mothers must forgo the use of power at the right
times. Dewey Daniels, in *I Never Loved Your Mind,* sees his parents as "plain, nice, detached, insignificant people." He likes them
and defends them against the arguments of Yvette, who hates
her parents. "The important thing," Dewey tells her, "is they leave
me alone and let me live my own life" (p. 47).

Similarly, Bobby Perkins—the hero of Zindel's *The Undertaker's Gone Bananas* and probably the most responsible and level-
headed of all the author's teenage protagonists—has parents who
know how to leave him alone. Bobby respects his father, "an
unrecognized gifted mathematician who deserves more than his
company ever paid him," and his mother, "a great lady" despite
her failure as an artist (pp. 38–39). He admires both because they
value recreational activities—mountain climbing and camping—
as well as intellectual pursuits. Bobby holds them in high esteem
especially because they are positive and hopeful people, even
though they lack material wealth (p. 40). Bobby also feels close
to his parents because they support him when he is in trouble;

they defend him when school officials cite him for hitting a class-mate who has disrupted a class Bobby likes (p. 13). But what really cements his relationship with them is their willingness to let him be alone. "The very best thing [Bobby] liked about his parents," the narrator says, "was any time they did take off, they didn't give him a big lecture on do's and don't's. All they would do is give him a big hug and say 'watch out for the milkman' " (p. 41). Bobby interprets this to mean that he should stay out of trouble. What is important to him is that his parents trust him to be alone, that they recognize his need to be on his own.

Zindel paints the school darker, satirizing teachers with a broad brush of disdain. Because of his own experience as a chemistry teacher, Zindel views the school through a distorted lens. Not one of his major protagonists likes school and thinks of it as a place to learn. And more than one of Zindel's teen characters has dropped out of high school. For them, the school is a social institution preoccupied with internal order and psychological fads and run by unintentionally comical teachers and administrators.

Dewey and Yvette in *I Never Loved Your Mind* are high school dropouts. Dewey quit because he found school "not urgent"; he "wasn't learning anything" (p. 6). Yvette complains, "The school I went to had a sixteen-foot fence around it. . . . my home eco-nomics teacher weighed 320 lbs. . . . my guidance teacher was divorced" (p. 14). Bobby Perkins in *Undertaker* strongly dislikes Fort Lee High School, a place he considers "a gigantic monument to man's attempt to educate his kids and his failure to do so" (p. 11). And the omniscient third-person narrator of *Pardon Me* crisply describes Edna's view of Curtis Lee High: "She didn't know whether she was enrolled in a school or a monkey sanatorium" (p. 30).

What makes these teenagers see school in such a negative light? Primarily, it's the faculty. Bobby Perkins in *Undertaker* claims that "only 25% of teachers know what they're doing." He tells Lauri, "They're not interested in what my ideas are. They shouldn't try to kill off my imagination" (p. 11). When he's challenged by Lauri, he does admit that there are some good teachers and that a large part of his problem is tactlessness. (Zindel is probably making a humorous reference to himself when he writes that

"Bobby's favorite teacher at school was a chemistry teacher who taught him how to apply his scientific procedures to real life" [p. 45].)

Nevertheless, it is clear that Zindel believes there are fewer good teachers than the twenty-five percent Bobby admits have merit. Over and over again, the author creates laughable caricatures of teachers. Mr. Zamborsky, the grade adviser and English teacher in *My Darling, My Hamburger* is constantly and stridently screaming for order (p. 2). As a dance monitor, he is ineffectual and foolish, blowing his whistle and barking out orders like "No smoking in the building. Do you hear me?" (p. 72). At graduation, with a whistle again, Mr. Zamborsky tries his sergeant routine: "Students! Make sure you're in the same place assigned at rehearsal. Boys on left side, girls on right side. Hurry!" (p. 155). Moreover, he's not only a buffoonish authority but also an incompetent teacher. He mistakes Sean's assignment essay on suicide as a "fascinating" writing exercise (p. 27) rather than recognizing it for what it really is—an outlet for suicidal thoughts and a plea for help from a confused adolescent. On Sean's term paper, "The Circus of Blackness," the English teacher writes: "You have a remarkable imagination. Very cryptic" (p. 153). Sean's "imagination" is actually a transparent analogy to his feelings of entrapment, and the one thing the essay isn't is cryptic.

In *Pardon Me*, Mr. Fettman—the teacher in charge of lunchroom monitoring—admittedly has a thankless job. He is not only ineffective as a policeman but is also a clownish victim of the cafeteria jungle. He's "too busy trying to figure out which kids [are] throwing grapes at him to notice a female student is always in some corner of the room kissing a different boy" (p. 21). He's also the target of students throwing pennies dipped in peanut butter (a colorful incident Zindel drew from his own teaching days on Staten Island).[5]

Teachers are also not exemplars of ethical behavior in Zindel's stories. Miss Conlin, the trusted faculty adviser of the Curtis Lee High School newspaper in *Pardon Me*, asks Edna to punch her out on the time clock so she can leave early for a play and not be docked. In fact, Edna and a classmate who works on the paper do this for their adviser three times a week. Aside from its impropriety, one also has to wonder what kind of school has teachers punching in and out like factory workers.

If the school is a factory, however, it is a strange and inefficient one. Marsh and Edna are classmates in Mr. Meizner's special class for "disturbed" students. The teacher-psychologist is pictured as a three-hundred-pound oaf who falls for every crazy story his students tell him. Almost every time they meet, Meizner has the students play sensitivity games, which he barely understands himself. With the song "The World Owes Us a Living" playing in the background, Meizner directs his charges to throw one of the group in the air and instructs another to catch their airborne classmate. His justification for the game is that it will instill trust. As Edna is thrown in the air, the psychologist chants, "Sing, everyone. Sing as we celebrate life for Edna. Trust us, Edna. We're your friends. Trust us, and listen to us sing." Understandably, Edna protests. "Shut up and trust," Meizner bellows (p. 124).

Zindel is not only satirizing the school here; he is also ridiculing the cult of pop psychology. Later in *Pardon Me,* at a party that eventually descends into chaos, a teenage evangelist named God Boy appears with a rock band and spouts the same claptrap as Meizner. "Sing," he coaxes the drunken teenagers. "You'll see only love. You will feel only truth. . . . raise your arms to the stars and let your song rise. . . . let your eyes explode with love. I want you to touch your Brothers and Sisters as you pass each other. Reach out your hand and touch each other. . . . If your clothes get in the way, take them off" (p. 214). Clothes, of course, always get in the way, so it is not surprising that love, trust, and truth are easily forgotten as the party ends in mayhem.

Zindel's skepticism about the relevance of the school and the competence of its officials can be seen in Edna's decision to bypass Meizner and anybody connected with the school when she seeks advice on how to help Marsh. (It is also significant that she ignores her parents.) Edna finally chooses to consult a witch who tells fortunes, and it is she who gives her the helpful advice she needs to begin to understand Marsh's problem (p. 152).

If the fortune teller is the very antithesis of establishment authority, then the police are the heart of this authority. When police appear in Zindel's young adult novels, they are depicted more negatively than either parents or teachers. Marsh claims, for example, that the police get paid off to ignore drinking places serving minors (p. 64). This may be bravado on his part, but he has no trouble ordering two drinks for himself and Edna. Either Marsh is correct or the police are derelict in enforcing the law.

In *Undertaker*, Bobby Perkins is picked up by the men in blue after a street fight at a block party and threatened with "everything from reform school to a bop on the head with a nightstick" (p. 15). When Lauri comes forth to exonerate him, the police let him go, but they continue to berate him with taunts like "What would your parents say?" and "You should be thrown out of school" (p. 17). It is interesting that Zindel has the police resort to falling back on the two other important adult authorities in the lives of teenagers; the police try to save face by appealing to parents and teachers as rightful holders of social authority. Later Bobby and Lauri give the police what they think is solid evidence that the man they are following has murdered his wife. But the police refuse to believe the story, partly because of Bobby's bad reputation and partly because of his tactlessness in calling them "jerks" (p. 94).

"You kids," the cops tell them, "think you can mug, kill, and freak out, and us [*sic*] cops are the ones that have to get stuck doing what your mothers and fathers should have done to you— beat the hell out of you when you were little runts" (pp. 99–100). As a powerless teenager, all Bobby feels he can do is resort to name-calling, while the police threaten him with the only thing Zindel thinks the police understand—force. That Bobby and Lauri turn out to be correct in their hypothesis about the murder only makes the police's position more untenable; they appear to be not only boorish but ineffectual and wrong.

The empty threats the police make in *Undertaker* turn into nightmarish reality in *Confessions*. Right after Chris and Lloyd witness the death of Lloyd's mother, Chris's mother, Helen, enters the house with three policemen to retrieve her son. She has brought the police with her to implicate Lloyd whom she hates. To Chris, two of the policemen look like "disgruntled orangutans," and the third officer looks like "Goliath" (p. 140). Lloyd is still in a state of shock over his mother's death, but all the policemen can do is allude to his strange life-style and imply he must be a child molester. They beat Lloyd and try to bribe him. His body and spirit totally shattered, Lloyd shoots himself to death when the police leave. Zindel here portrays the police as insensitive and brutal accomplices in the suicide as well as representative of the societal authority that had long condemned Lloyd for his unorthodox way of life.

Parents, teachers, and the police, Zindel thinks, often misuse and abuse their power, disappointing and disillusioning teenagers. Despite these unappealing caricatures of power, Zindel also rejects and even satirizes those characters who repudiate social authority altogether (Yvette in *I Never Loved Your Mind* and God Boy in *Pardon Me,* for example). Zindel's attitude toward social order is similar to the viewpoint expressed by Dewey Daniels in *I Never Loved Your Mind.* Disenchanted by an adult world he finds pretentious and unjust and hurt by Yvette whom he has tried to love, Dewey decides it is in his own interests to accept the basic underpinnings of society. Philosophically, Dewey concludes, he's "not going to give civilization a kick in the behind because [he] might need an appendectomy sometime" (p. 181).

Dewey therefore affirms—and Zindel believes—that one must accept authority with an open mind and open eyes. To paraphrase any number of political philosophers, the only thing worse than parents, teachers, and police is the lack of them.

8. Fathers and Mothers, Boys and Girls

"Are you a sexist?"

When librarian Audrey Eaglen, during an interview with Zindel in 1978, asked this provocative question, she was probably thinking of the fictional characters in his young adult novels. On the one hand, innocuous fathers are overshadowed by their neurotic wives; on the other hand, teenage males dominate as the major protagonists.

Zindel's elliptical response to this pointed question referred not to his characterizations but to his own immediate life. "As I observe my son and daughter as infants," he commented, "I see great differences. Our home is unisex. I am open to everything my kids want to do, including choice of career. My initial observation, however, as a sort of a new parent, is that David will be more qualified to unload refrigerators at a GE factory than Lizabeth."[1]

It is appropriate that Zindel answered this question about his fictional characters by looking at his own life because his experiences have been the greatest influence on the substance of his characterizations. "Sexism," though, is not an accurate word to describe his attitudes toward males and females in his young adult novels. He doesn't believe in or justify discriminatory behavior, but he does depict his male and female characters with distinct gender identities.

The adult characters reflect Zindel's bad experiences with his own parents and his former teaching colleagues. In the very few instances where he has created sets of "perfect" parents, there are almost no differences between mothers and fathers. They are both so blandly depicted, in fact, that they are interchangeable and equally lacking in credibility. In most of Zindel's novels for teenagers, however, the adults are dark figures. His caricatures of mothers are the stuff of nightmares: they are eccentric, alcoholic, schizophrenic, compulsive, loveless, physically debilitated, prone to stealing, dishonest, overbearing. The negative features of Zindel's fictional fathers are less extreme: they are hypocritical, distrustful, paranoic. In many of the stories the fathers are dead or missing and only a memory for the protagonists. There are certainly no destructive father figures comparable to Schizoid Suzy or the mothers of Lloyd, Edna, and Chris—whose parenting styles are respectively emasculating, smothering, and domineering. The mother is *the* controlling parent and one of the primary sources of trouble for their offspring. Similarly, Zindel portrays male teachers as mindless and laughable fools (like Mr. Zamborsky in *My Darling*) and the female teachers as devious and aware of their incompetence (like Miss Conlin in *Pardon Me*).

He treats his adolescent main characters very differently. First of all, they are developed with empathy and understanding. The character weaknesses they exhibit are part of their adolescence, not their personalities. Second, the male protagonists play more commanding roles in the stories than their female counterparts. The boys are assertive, imaginative, intelligent, rebellious, and impulsive; the girls are generally less self-confident, less decisive, and less imaginative. The task assigned to Zindel's teenage heroines is usually to complement (and compliment) the male's character strengths and to help protect him from the excesses of his own abilities. Even in *Pardon Me,* the one novel in which the girl is a stronger character than her male partner, it is Edna's function in the story to help Marsh purge himself of his debilitating hangups. And in the many Zindel novels featuring a teenage hero-

heroine duo, the female's main role is to provide friendship to her stronger partner and to help him when he needs help. This doesn't mean that the author treats his heroines as objects. They are distinct personalities in their own right, and they—like their male companions—are changed for the better by their experiences in the story. But their role is subservient to the males.

The only novel (other than collaborations) that Zindel wrote with a solitary female lead character is *The Girl Who Wanted a Boy*. In it he has endowed Sibella with skills traditionally considered to be the exclusive province of males; she is handy with tools and is an excellent television repair technician. But, Zindel reminds us early in the story, "she was somewhat limited in physics. . . . she knew that running a Mobil Gas Station was a more realistic goal than heading up something like the laboratory at the Mount Palomar Observatory" (p. 8). In addition to her intellectual limitations and insecurities, Sibella feels unequal to the task of satisfying the social expectations of her older sister and mother. Her divorced mother makes a career of finding boyfriends and her mindless sister, Maureen—who is living with a boyfriend of her own—tries to get Sibella into the sexual fast lane. Although influenced by her mother's way of life and her sister's pressures, Sibella has more discerning thoughts: she wants to pick up a boy who not only looks "delicious" but also could be "tender" (p. 11).

She finally settles on Dan, a garage mechanic and self-admitted bum. Despite his persistent objections, Sibella pursues him relentlessly. "I want to help you, Dan," she tells him. "I want to devote my life to you, to help you reach the pinnacle of your chosen career. Whatever your dream, I'll help it come true" (p. 55). She tells her father she wants to "own Dan" (p. 117). And she spends her entire savings to buy him the van of his dreams. She does this even though she knows that Dan is going to leave her. "At least one of us got their dream," she tells her dream boy (p. 137).

Zindel has created Sibella as a girl with unusual skills and a discriminating nature. Yet she is obsessed with finding the perfect boy—the dream that is the stereotypical fantasy of teenage girlhood. Sibella goes about her search in a unique way and with a special passion, but that does not alter the fact that she views her role in life very conventionally—to be subservient to the male, to help *him* reach *his* goal. This constitutes the measure of her success in life. When it does not work, she falls into the depths of despair, even contemplating suicide for a while. But upon realizing how many other people care for her, she begins to be more reasonable about her disappointment. Still, she craves the answer to the secret of love: "Why did God or nature or whoever it was give such powerful feelings to any young girl? To me? To all young girls?" (p. 146).

I Never Loved Your Mind presents another side of Zindel's sex-role stereotyping. When Dewey first meets alienated hippie Yvette Goethals, it is clear to the reader that she is a hypocrite. She professes love for all life, yet she shows disdain for all people. She wants the respect of those for whom she works, yet she unashamedly steals from the hospital. On one level, Yvette is a manipulative, untrustworthy, illiterate girl who distracts and seduces a self-involved innocent. On another level, as James Henke argues, Yvette is an earth mother who represents the goddess of fertility and rebirth.[2] She at first coyly rejects Dewey's inexperienced overtures to her, turning down gifts of flowers and candy. When Dewey catches on, he offers her a fifty-pound bag of radish seed—and Yvette seduces him. "I felt like I had just been born," Dewey ruminates in the afterglow of his lovemaking (p. 124). But to Yvette, it was "no more than a roll in the hay." "To us," she explains to Dewey, "that's like burping" (p. 156). Being a symbol of the "Natural World" as well as of the "Higher Consciousness," Yvette spurns Dewey's love because to her, he is corrupted by civilization. "I never loved your mind," Yvette screams back at him as she rides off into the sunset with her hippie entourage (p. 176).

As a two-faced, exploitative girl, Yvette not only fails to support Dewey; she plays with him and hurts him. She takes his money instead of going on a date with him; she sleeps with him and then drops him without feeling. And, as the archetypical earth mother, Yvette is crudely anti-intellectual. She is illiterate and emotionally unresponsive. She represents the animal in the natural world and the mindless in the human world.

The only symbolic male character in Zindel's stories is Jason in *Harry and Hortense at Hormone High*—but he leaves the scene with considerably more dignity than Yvette does. Jason fancies himself to be Icarus, who in Greek mythology died when he flew too near the sun. He indulges in this fantasy because he cannot accept an awful truth in his life: his father murdered his mother and then committed suicide. Zindel makes Jason a tragic hero, someone—like Icarus—who is fated to kill himself. But in this story, Jason is more than a tool of the gods. Zindel fashions him into a prophet preaching a message of love and understanding in the den of iniquity called Hormone High. He dies a senseless death, but to Harry and Hortense, Jason does not die in vain. Because of him they vow to dedicate their lives to fight against evil.

Yvette is deceitful, harsh, bitter, overbearing, and insensitive; Jason is innocent, sensitive, well intentioned, and trusting. These contrasts—male versus female symbols, Greek god as savior versus earth mother as witch—are a microcosm of how Zindel uses gender characteristics.

But is he a sexist? No, for he believes that the Davids and Lizabeths of the world should have equal opportunity to be what they want to be. He also has set ideas about males and females, however—who they are, what they act like, what they are capable of. These ideas transcend his comment about David being more likely to work in a refrigerator plant than his sister. Zindel, it seems, believes that males are *weaker* than females because it is the men who abandon their families, who require the emotional support and direction of women, and who are passive victims of dominating mothers. Females are more aggressive, in Zindel's young adult novels. Depending on their inclinations, his feminine characters are either the crusher or the savior of men. In this inversion of the traditional stereotype, females give and males receive.

Why, then, are readers left with more positive views of males?

The main reason is that Zindel creates his female characters almost always in relation to the males they help or hurt. When Edna helps Marsh overcome his neurosis about his father's death in *Pardon Me,* when Lorraine helps John through his alcohol and gambling compulsions in the *Pigman* novels, when Chris's mother so dominates her son that he can't even go to the bathroom without a comment from her in *Confessions,* and when an independent Dewey is reduced to an abject follower by illiterate Yvette in *I Never Loved Your Mind,* one can see that women and girls are defined by their connection to young men. As helpmate or spoiler, the female in Zindel's young adult novels is rarely more than an exciting and memorable agent.

9. The Inevitable Adventure: A Matter of Life and Death

Harry and Hortense at Hormone High expresses Paul Zindel's deep concern about our civilization—a culture he believes has turned in on itself, reveling in self-gratification and self-glorification. In an interview with Aidan Chambers, Zindel states: "You could refer to it as god dying. . . . As the gods die, their civilization begins to die." Then he turns to what he perceives is a contemporary preoccupation with death. "I am amused by critics," he observes, "who say that our great spate of death books and death plays are really artistic coverings for an inability of men to communicate with each other." Feeling it is self-deception and a rationalization, he takes issue with this view. "I think," he concludes, "these books about death are really about death."[1]

This pessimism about the direction in which our civilization is heading may be the reason Zindel makes death a visible topic in many of his young adult novels. Ironically, though, his treatment of death is not really about death. It is used as a counterpoint to Zindel's affirmation of life and love—the prime messages of his stories.

How does Zindel depict death? The clearest view is found in *The Pigman's Legacy*. Death is seen as a formidable obstacle at the end of "the game of life"—as a "wall as thick as eternity and as high as eternity" stretching "as far to the left and to the right

as eternity" (p. 68). The colonel, slowly dying himself, asks John
to play the game of life. "I'm trying to smash the wall, but I can't,"
he tells the colonel when he is confronted in the game by this
metaphorical barrier. The colonel interprets this to mean: "When
it comes time for you to die, you will fight against it with all your
might. . . . you will do everything possible to escape it" (p. 69).
Later in the same story, Dolly, the lunchroom cleaning woman,
also plays the game of life, but her response to the wall of death
is quite different. "I [would] fall down on my knees and kiss it,"
she decides (p. 137). Dolly attributes this response to her religious
upbringing, implying not a desire for death but an acceptance of
it. Both John and Dolly show courage in the face of death, but
John sees it as an enemy, and Dolly looks at it as the inevitable
end of life.

The surety of death was recognized three years earlier in *The
Pigman*. As he witnesses the sudden termination of Mr. Pignati's
life, John envisions his own demise—"the cold tiles, the draft that
moved about me, the nice solid fact that someday I was going to
end up in a coffin myself" (p. 178). And the inescapable perma-
nence of death is further established by Zindel in *The Pigman's
Legacy* when the colonel foreshadows his own end with this
thought: "I had this vision that I was being nailed inside of a
coffin. My feet and arms were immobile. There was nothing I
could do to get out of it" (p. 165).

The end to the game of life is given a somewhat different thrust
in *The Undertaker's Gone Bananas*. Waiting for her friend Bobby,
Lauri thinks back to a class talk she had once given about her
horror at seeing a childhood playmate burned to death before her
eyes. Trying to come to terms with this traumatic event, she had
begun her talk by quoting an anonymous "someone": "death is
not a foe, but an inevitable adventure" (p. 178). A loose inter-
pretation of this aphorism might be: don't be afraid of death, don't
fight against it, and don't let it become an obsession that can
distract you from enjoying the adventure of life.

It is this adventure that *The Undertaker's Gone Bananas* illustrates. Bobby and Lauri, in their dogged pursuit of a mortician
they suspect of murder, are brought face to face with death—

represented by Mr. Hulka, the undertaker—as an evil force in life. Until they discover the bizarre truth, they guess that the mortician was caught in a love triangle; when his wife discovered the affair, they suppose, Hulka murdered her. Lauri, however, sees herself and Bobby in a dangerous triangle themselves, with Death as the third party. Ever since the fire tragedy, she had been obsessively afraid of death. Now, deeply entangled with a fearless Bobby in a dangerous adventure to uncover Hulka's crime, Lauri loses her phobia. All she can think of is Bobby's safety and her own blossoming romantic feelings for him. "Please, Bobby," she silently pleads, "just not being afraid of dying isn't enough to make life worthwhile. I think I'm ready for the next step" (p. 187). But Bobby is not quite ready to respond because "the inevitable adventure" has not been confronted completely. Only after the fearless teenager (with Lauri's help) captures Hulka redhanded is he ready to reciprocate Lauri's feelings with a kiss. And Lauri, having overcome a paralyzing fear of death by gaining a victory over the death forces in life, kisses Bobby passionately, whispering a well-known excerpt from Andrew Marvell's poem "To His Coy Mistress": "The grave's a fine and private place, But none, I think do there embrace" (p. 239).

Juxtaposing the themes of death and love is something Zindel does again and again in his books. For instance, he uses the cemetery as the setting for a scene in *Harry and Hortense* in which the two teenagers come to terms with the tragedy of their friend's death. Having just attended Jason's funeral, Harry and Hortense stay at the cemetery until everyone else has gone in order to do a postmortem on their fallen hero's life and death, vowing to dedicate their lives to deeds of importance. And something more: "I was beginning to feel very much alone," Harry recalls, "but then as soon as I *felt* alone, Hortense reached over and took my hand. . . . We still sat on the cold cement bench in front of the tomb, but at least we were together" (p. 147). With death all around, this "fine and private place" becomes the setting for romance—and the site of the two promising to revive a dying civilization.

Despite the many Zindel characters who are concerned with

breathing life into dying people, "revival" is not Zindel's message to his readers. Dewey is an inhalation therapist in *I Never Loved Your Mind,* but he faints in his first attempt at reviving someone (and wakes up in the morgue). Rod Gittens is also an inhalation therapist in *My Darling, My Hamburger,* but he is an unfeeling, manipulative predator who tries to rape Liz on a date. And Chris's mother, a nurse in *Confessions,* at best performs a holding action in keeping Lloyd's mother barely alive. Even more to the point, her suffocating control over her son metaphorically siphons life-giving air from him.

What Zindel is concerned with is not reviving others but reviving oneself. He places death in so many of his young adult novels in order for teenagers to learn the value of life and love from the death of others. Marsh Mellow is a hopeless schizophrenic and eccentric recluse until he faces the reality of his father's death. John and Lorraine come to express their love for each other only after the Pigman and the colonel die. Chris feels, for the first time, his own person only after the painful death of Lloyd's mother and the shattering suicide of Lloyd.

Zindel himself, therefore, appears to be that "someone" whom Lauri quotes as the author of "death is not a foe, but an inevitable adventure." To Zindel, death is not just "a wall of eternity" at the end of life. It is a lesson, which, properly understood, will give teenage observers—and readers of Zindel's stories—a new perspective on life.

10. Dialogue, Humor, and Metaphor: Patterns of Style

In Paul Zindel's writing formula, discussed in chapter 2, the thread tying together the ten guidelines is his emphasis on avoiding boredom for his young readers. "Hey, kids," the author tells his audience in effect, "I recognize how boring Shakespeare and other brilliant writers can be when you're so young and not ready to plumb the great passions of Life."[1] This overriding concern with keeping his teenage readers always interested helps explain some distinctive features of his writing: his use of the first-person narrative or third-person omniscient narrative, his reliance on lively dialogue, his liberal employment of literary devices and gimmicks, and his repetitive patterns of animal metaphors.

To tell his stories through the eyes of the teenager, Zindel uses two narrative points of view exclusively—the first person and the omniscient third person. In the first sentence of both *The Pigman* and *Pardon Me,* readers learn that John Conlan and Marsh Mellow hate school: John informs readers directly in the first person ("Now I don't like school . . ."), and Marsh's thoughts are communicated through a third-person narrator ("Marsh Mellow was fifteen years old and hated almost everything about Curtis Lee High School").

In a review typifying what others have said about Zindel's young adult novels, *Publishers Weekly* wrote that *My Darling, My Ham-*

burger is "told with such compassionate and loving awareness that the reader is swept immediately into the illusion that no outsider is recording the story"; the characters, the review continues, appear to be "talking it out loud themselves."[2] *My Darling* is not a first-person narrative; it is told in the third person by an omniscient narrator. The way Zindel creates the illusion "that no outsider is recording the story" is by embellishing the narration with italicized diary entries and interior monologues. Readers are therefore privy not only to actions and dialogue but also to private thoughts and fantasies of the main characters.

To heighten and sustain interest, Zindel almost always tells his stories from the vantage points of at least two characters. Although he uses the first-person narrative to keep his readers close to the characters, Zindel believes that this point of view has an inherent weakness—boredom.[3] By varying the characters who relate the story, the author creates a narrative situation that can appeal to a wider audience than if only one person were describing the action. In the two *Pigman* novels, for instance, those readers who are put off by John Conlan's arrogance and sarcasm still have a chance of being pulled into the story by Lorraine, who tells her more thoughtful version of the events in alternate chapters. The third-person narrator in *Undertaker* creates the same effect. Readers are privy to both Bobby's and Lauri's interior monologues as well as the exterior action of the plot.

Closely related to Zindel's preference for the first-person narrative and the omniscient third-person narrative is his reliance on dialogue to create characters, set narrative flow, and carry plot action. "I have a general boredom with description," Zindel says. "I'm not interested too much in what a room looks like. I am very interested in what people are saying to each other."[4] From the first time that John and Lorraine talk to Mr. Pignati, it is clear that the conversations between the two teenagers and the Pigman are the instruments in the novel that define the characters and tell the story. Similarly, the dialogues between Chris and Lloyd in *Confessions* and between Edna and Marsh in *Pardon Me* communicate a great deal of the plot action and sketch the primary character development. A conversational tone so marks Zindel's first-person narratives that the novels are, in a very real sense, dialogues with the reader. For example, both Dewey Daniels in *I Never Loved Your Mind* and Harry in *Harry and Hortense at Hormone High* immediately launch into the second person as they try to convince the reader of their identity of interests. And they do this in such a style that their personality traits very quickly become clear to those reading the novels. Dewey's alliteration, obnoxious footnotes, and misused Latinized words reveal an insolent, pretentious, and insecure dropout. Harry's wide-eyed sincerity and seriousness are noticeable right from his beginning appeal to readers: "Jason Rohr was a boy who changed our lives. He's gone now, but I feel it's my duty to write down all that he taught us, so that in case you're sitting in a classroom thinking your life . . . is a big sad crock, we want you to know about Jason because what he told us might help" (p. 3).

The language of the dialogues—those among the characters and those between the first-person narrator and the reader—is so important to Zindel that he sometimes dictates it into a tape recorder twice at different stages of his writing to "protect its sound and to make sure it doesn't become too wordy."[5] He believes "the language must give an appearance of being contemporary and yet not go out of date."[6]

To ensure that readers think that "no outsider is recording the story," Zindel utilizes various devices that break up the linear print and "give an appearance of being contemporary." Sixteen years separated his writing of *The Pigman* and *Harry and Hortense at Hormone High,* but both novels employ the same literary devices. John Conlan, for instance, displays his best graffiti output, and Harry meticulously reproduces Jason Rohr's public letters to his classmates ending with a large handwritten "Icarus, a god." The two hero-heroine pairs—John and Lorraine and Harry and Hortense—write letters signed in their distinctive signatures, and the missives between Maggie and Liz in *My Darling, My Hamburger* are scrawled in their own handwriting. Official school memos and correspondence add a degree of authenticity to *My Darling.* Drawings and doodles illustrating games John and Lorraine play with Mr. Pignati clarify the didactic nature of the games and are entertaining sideshows for the reader. And John's euphemistic use of "@#$%" (with appropriate variations) to indicate curses and Dewey's interminable footnotes reflect the characters Zindel is portraying and also help pull readers into the story.

All these devices support Zindel's blueprint for writing the young adult novel. He is just as methodical in applying humor to his stories. Zindel admits that his humor is best characterized by the term *bathos,* which usually begins on a relatively high plane of seriousness and quickly descends to a trivial level. One way he has incorporated this type of hyperbole into his stories is "by taking what appears to be an established word and fracturing it with what seems to be an unlikely word."[7] Consider, for example, the titles *Confessions of a Teenage Baboon, The Undertaker's Gone Bananas,* and *My Darling, My Hamburger.* Serious old-fashioned words like *confessions, undertaker,* and *darling* are juxtaposed with incongruous terms, amusing the reader and arousing curiosity about the novels. In *Harry and Hortense at Hormone High,* Zindel has embellished his word humor with alliteration, accentuating the comic appeal of the book.

Another characteristic of all of Zindel's young adult novels is the inclusion of jokes, riddles, and puns liberally sprinkled throughout the stories. In *I Never Loved Your Mind,* Zindel indicates Dewey Daniels's intellectual pretention and brash cuteness through word humor like the following:

- *Riddles*
  Q: What do people see in sado-masochism?
  A: It beats me. (p. 64)

- *One-liners*
  "I think one of the reasons [we embalm bodies] is to make sure who ends up in a coffin doesn't sit up during the wake." (p. 7)

- *Puns*
  "The guidance teacher at my old school called me down once and asked what career I was going to undertake, and I told her undertaking." (p. 15)

To find these and other examples of word humor, Zindel acknowledges that he sometimes consults joke books with such titles as *Two Thousand Insults.*[8] And, indeed, the sharp edge and exaggerated nature of his humor often put his jokes into the realm of insults, either as sarcasm or as satire. Speaking about his parents' inability to communicate or relate to each other, John Conlan in *The Pigman's Legacy* indulges in one of his frequent sarcastic outbursts: "My father and mother never even touch each other, which makes me wonder how on earth I was ever born. I figure it was an accident—they both happened to be walking around the bedroom nude and they made a mistake and tripped" (p. 111). In a similar vein, Harry in *Harry and Hortense* satirizes his mother: "When my mother prepares meat loaf, she looks like a woman trying to beat an abalone, and she throws a lot of parsley, onion, and Hamburger Helper into the thing so that by the time it hits the dinner table, it looks like a souvenir from the petrified forest" (p. 61).

Zindel also manipulates words in naming characters, usually to cast aspersions on them. In *Pardon Me,* one of a trio of girls who "practically threw [their bodies] at every guy on the football team" (p. 194) is named Joan Hybred—which is a combination of *hybrid, hymen, crossbred,* and who knows what else? The cast of minor characters in the same novel includes many with appropriately descriptive names, such as Lucille Bore and Chris Phlegm. (It also includes a character named Bonnie Hilderstraw, whose name echoes that of the author's wife, Bonnie Hildebrand.) Gertrude Bang in *Confessions* and Norma Jean Stapleton in *Pardon Me* are sexually loose and unattractive girls who win pigs as door prizes at parties; Marilyn Monroe's real name was Norma Jean Baker and Stapleton was the community in which Zindel's parents grew up. Mr. Brightenbach is a physics teacher in *The Girl Who Wanted a Boy* and Mr. Herbert is a chemistry teacher in the same story; television's Mister Wizard's real surname is Herbert. Rod Gittens—which is a word play on *good riddance*—is an obnoxious minor character in *My Darling.*

Zindel is just as playful or cleverly caustic in naming some of his antagonists and protagonists. Mr. Hulka is the monstrous mortician in *The Undertaker's Gone Bananas;* Lloyd Dipardi is a tragic figure who puts on wild parties to cover up his unhappiness and commits suicide at the end of *Confessions* (Dipardi = Die + Party); Marsh Mellow, the name of the troubled hero in *Pardon Me,* carries with it a host of images—a boy with a soft center, a boy sinking in a marsh, a boy who is unperturbed by the exterior world because he is so confused by his own life, and so on.

Although Zindel is not Jewish, he likens his humor to that of Woody Allen. It is "a New York type of humor," he says, dominated by "the vulnerable person who feels constantly at the mercy of the fates and of everybody around him."[9] Thus, Dewey Daniels meets with little success when he chases Yvette Goethals (in *I Never Loved Your Mind:* "I kissed her neck gently. She was staring out at the blinking lights of the shoreline and she reflexively wiped her neck quite like brushing off a nibbling mosquito" (p. 87).

Much of the time, however, Zindel directs his humorous barbs at others, and it resembles Rodney Dangerfield's ridicule and put-downs more than Woody Allen's self-effacing jabs. Talking to a school counselor about her daughter, Edna Shinglebox's mother in *Pardon Me* complains, "No matter what she does, she screws it up. She went to a picnic and came back with a tick in her ear. I take her to Macy's and her hair gets caught in the escalators" (p. 9). In the same novel, Marsh thinks of his alcoholic mother as "Lady Macbeth with half a load on," and comments, "All she seemed to do was run around the house all day in her polka-dot nightgown, with her long, graying hair flowing down her back, and watch news reports while sipping her diet beer and opening up cans of sardines. . . . She could make a fortune endorsing shampoos by saying how, whenever she used a certain shampoo her hair felt alive, and then they could just show a shot of her and everyone would think it was Medusa" (p. 10).

The most common technique Zindel uses to ridicule his characters is to match them with animal metaphors and similes. Mr. Hulka's moving men in *Undertaker,* to Bobby Perkins's imaginative mind, "looked like a trio of pre-humanoid creatures . . .

three hairy apes" (p. 3). Later Bobby's girlfriend Lauri mockingly describes an apartment policeman she calls Joe the Schmo as someone "pounding his chest in rage, drooling like a dragon that had lost its prey" (p. 136). In *Confessions,* Chris informs his readers that two of the cops about to beat up Lloyd Dipardi look like "disgruntled orangutans" (p. 140). Marsh Mellow, in *Pardon Me,* after he brands his mother with the name of Schizoid Suzy, caricatures Mr. Spooner, his next-door neighbor, as a "gorilla that used to tour with the Ringley Bros. circus" (p. 11). And cafeteria food in Marsh's school, we are told, is served on a plate that "looked like it was the final resting place for a stuffed roast rodent" (p. 31). Although it may offend the sensibilities of adults and some teenagers, this kind of derogatory slapstick has a special appeal to adolescent readers, especially when it is directed against the symbols of established society with which Zindel's reading audience is in conflict.

On another level, however, Zindel's fondness for animal metaphors and similes reflects a more serious purpose than mindless ad hominem attacks. The author often utilizes these devices to express two related ideas: the inherent animal character of human beings and their inability to communicate with one another. One metaphor Zindel frequently uses is that of the zoo; in *The Pigman* it is a pervasive symbol. Until Mr. Pignati meets John and Lorraine, the zoo is the home of his only friend, a baboon named Bobo. The zoo is also the place where the two teenagers meet the Pigman for an attempted reconciliation after they wreck his house and valued possessions. And it is the place where Mr. Pignati has his fatal heart attack after he learns that Bobo has died. On her first visit to the zoo, Lorraine encounters hostile attendants, is attacked by a peacock wanting her peanuts, and sees graphic pictures of bats "sucking the blood out of a horse's neck while the horse was sleeping" (p. 59). What truly upsets her, though, is meeting a strange ten-year-old boy who stares at her "as though [she] was a bat in a cage and he was on the outside looking in at me" (p. 59). To Zindel, the zoo here is a prison for man and animal—a symbol, as critic James Henke says, "of the plight of modern man in an impersonal society, where we live in a cage of indifference, boredom, or self-absorption . . . in close proximity but not together."[10]

Zindel may have adapted this metaphor from *The Zoo Story,* the first play of Edward Albee, who was a major influence on the author when he attended Wagner College. In that play, a transient named Jerry meets Peter, an established publishing executive, on a park bench and tries to explain why he feels so alienated from society and why visiting the zoo has clarified for him the meaning of his isolation in the world: "I went to the zoo to find out more about the way people exist with animals and the way animals exist with one another and with people too. It probably wasn't a fair test, what with everyone separated by bars from everyone else."[11] Isolated from one another by barriers, people and animals in the zoo pursue their own interests and no one is able to communicate with anyone else.

Zindel also uses the zoo metaphor to portray a scene or situation that is out of control and that has no redeeming value. In *The Amazing and Death-Defying Diary of Eugene Dingman,* the employee cafeteria at the Lake Henry resort simulates a zoo—and in fact is called "the zoo." On his way to breakfast the first morning, the fifteen-year-old is swept along "a paved path filled with a rushing horde of employees dressed in uniforms." It looks to Eugene like "a march of mutant Amazon ants" (p. 14). When he finally arrives at "the zoo," he finds "a hundred workers eating in an area the size of a portable classroom." And what they are eating is little better than animal food—"fried eggs that looked like cyclops eyes, cold toast with congealed orange marmalade, decaying coffee, and pork sausages in the shape of fried fingers." "I don't want to write anything more about the zoo," Eugene notes after this description, "or my diary will be endangered by uncontrollable reverse peristalsis" (p. 15).

The most bizarre and destructive actions in situations that are out of control usually occur at parties, where the teenage characters seem to lose the dignity and sanity distinguishing them from the buffoonish adult world which Zindel repeatedly parodies. John and Lorraine are accomplices in destroying the Pigman's house as a result of their unchaperoned party in the old man's home. Total chaos occurs in *Pardon Me* when drunken orgies cause a fire that engulfs the large house where the party is being held, resulting in the death of Marsh's pet raccoon. And in *Confessions,* a riotous party put on by Lloyd Dipardi precedes and influences the tragic events bringing the novel to a climax.

Why is a party so important to Zindel? "A party and teenagers are synonymous," the author asserts. "It is the meeting place where the social mettle of each kid is put to its highest test. Parties are serious business, and kids find out who they are there." If this is true, then Zindel's teenage characters must feel badly defeated; the "kids" have failed their "highest test." John and Lorraine, Marsh and Edna, and Chris do nothing to stop the parties' destructive course. At best, they are marginal to it, and they survive. "No matter what their actual behavior," Zindel adds, "they're all sort of hoping they'll be liked or at least noticed."[12] Zindel's protagonists fail on this level, too. They make no new friends and are noticed only by their old friends or by those who mock them. The real reason for the parties, Zindel admits, is "to create an electric confusion in which a false growth has taken place—a substitute device for a genuine epiphany."[13]

In this plot device, Zindel has created a diversion that allows his characters to make radical changes in thought and action, leading ultimately to the story's climax. The party, then, is Zindel's "magic box"—a shortcut to character and plot development. The party's "electric confusions," for example, permit John and Lorraine to shed their narrow focus on satisfying their immediate needs and to begin to think about the consequences of their actions. The "electric confusions" also cause Marsh to lose the protection of his pet raccoon and to team up with Edna who helps him come to terms with his past. The party is therefore an important component of Zindel's novels not because it provides "a testing ground" for the teenagers but because it satisfies the author's overriding desire not to bore his readers and his need to bring the stories to a quick climax by resolving the problems of his protagonists.

Zindel has used a variety of literary devices in his young adult novels, and from them, he has created patterns of style that some critics may find irritating because of their repetitiveness and transparency. But even Shakespeare and other brilliant writers were criticized in their day for manipulative literary contrivances, derivative plots, and farcical humor; they, too, were accused of catering to their audiences. It is, however, largely an academic question, since Zindel seems to have succeeded in applying his elements of style to attain his primary goal—keeping his audience reading.

11. The Young Adult Novel and Zindel's Future

A good measure of a young adult novelist's success is the length of time the original hard-cover edition of a novel stays in print. Few such editions written for teenagers today are in print longer than three years; those that are reprinted in paperback last perhaps another five years. The hard-cover edition of every young adult novel that Zindel has ever written is still in print, even *The Pigman* twenty years after its original publication. Just as remarkable is the fact that all his fiction for teenagers is available in at least one paperback edition. And in December 1987 Zindel concluded an agreement with Bantam Publishers which guarantees that all of his young adult novels (including the one he is now writing) will be in paperback until the year 2003.

Success like this is difficult to argue with, but it is questionable whether the coming generation of teenage readers will have a new crop of Zindel novels to entertain them. At the present, Zindel is finishing an eleventh young adult novel, tentatively titled *A Begonia for Miss Applebaum,* and scheduled for publication by Harper in the spring of 1989, in which he plans for the first time to use his experiences with his son and daughter to develop the characters of a pair of teenage protagonists whom he has named Max and Zelda.[1] He also plans to have a major adult character die as his mother did. Zindel, however, says he feels limited by the constraints of the genre and that this may be his last fiction for teenagers because he wishes to strive for something new.

By its very nature, Zindel thinks that the young adult novel "has to function as a rite of passage in which the hero's naïveté is changed by the learning of an uncomplex lesson." In this lesson-learning, the author has explored the basic needs of life, which he identifies as fivefold: the need to be admired, the need for sexual satisfaction, the need to be loved, the need to have a purpose, and the need for trust. Zindel's aim is to examine these essentials of existence with "more vigor and less timidity" than he has previously done. The problem, he says, is that the genre of the young adult novel imposes on him the necessity of simple language and a treatment lacking depth and breadth—restrictions that he thinks will not allow him to accomplish his goal.

He wants to write more plays partly because he sees himself as a playwright by nature and partly because he believes drama offers him the freedom to attain his objective. As this is written, he is putting the final touches on a play he has worked on for several years. The drama, currently titled *Destiny on Half-Moon Street,* turns on the themes of sexuality and loving and explores in more depth and with more openness some of the characters he developed in *Confessions of a Teenage Baboon.* Having passed the age of fifty, however, Zindel looks at other playwrights and finds that by that age most had exhausted their creative energies. He is a little skeptical, therefore, about the likelihood of his achieving his new artistic goals; nevertheless, he still feels he hasn't peaked yet.

The main reason for his reappraisal and cautious optimism is that Zindel thinks he has finally outgrown his adolescence. Like his teenage heroes and heroines, he used to see himself as a "victim of a cruel world," a "vulnerable and fragile figure." This limited view of himself, he insists, has prevented him from examining "the lofty aspects of the human spirit." But having worked through personal hurts and family conflicts in his young adult novels, conveying important lessons to his readers and to himself, Paul Zindel has come of age. He now feels ready to express what he says is "the greatest vision of heaven I can have."

Will this mean an end to his career as a young adult novelist? A new beginning as a playwright or as a serious novelist for adults? With admirable candor and a healthy sense of humor, Zindel says he is not sure, but he wants to achieve "a sense of purpose and honesty." And he adds, "If I can't make any of this work, I hope I have the extra good sense to hang it all up and go tarpon fishing."

Fishing, however, is not what Eugene Dingman means at the end of his diary when he quotes Albert Camus: "In the midst of winter, I finally learned there was in me an invincible summer" (p. 214). At this point, the young diarist writes, "Eugene Dingman born." And Paul Zindel has just learned another lesson.

Appendix: Honors and Prizes Awarded Paul Zindel's Books and Plays

Young Adult Novels

Confessions of a Teenage Baboon
  Best Books for Young Adults, 1977, American Library Association

I Never Loved Your Mind
  Outstanding Children's Books of 1970, *New York Times*

My Darling, My Hamburger
  Outstanding Children's Books of 1969, *New York Times*

Pardon Me, You're Stepping on My Eyeball
  Best Books for Young Adults, 1976, American Library Association

The Pigman
  Best of the Best Young Adult Books, 1960–74, American Library Association
  Outstanding Children's Books of 1968, *New York Times*
  Boston Globe–Horn Book Award, 1969

The Pigman's Legacy
  Best Books for Young Adults, 1980, American Library Association

Plays

The Effect of Gamma Rays on Man-in-the-Moon Marigolds
  Pulitzer Prize in Drama, 1971
  Best of the Best Books for Young Adults, 1970–83, American Library
    Association
  Obie Award, 1970
  New York Critics Award, 1971
  Vernon Rice Drama Desk Award, 1971
  Notable Books of 1971, American Library Association

Notes and References

Chapter 1

1. *The Amazing and Death-Defying Diary of Eugene Dingman* (New York, 1987), p. 2; pages hereafter cited in text.
2. Paul Zindel, interview, 3 May 1987.
3. Paul Zindel, "The Magic of Special People," *School Media Quarterly,* Fall 1979, p. 31.
4. Audrey Eaglen, "Of Life, Death, Kids, and Inhalation Therapy: An Interview with Paul Zindel," *Top of the News,* Winter 1978, p. 183.
5. Zindel, interview, 17 May 1987.
6. Zindel, interview, 3 May 1987.
7. Ibid.
8. *Current Biography* (New York, 1973), p. 445.
9. Zindel, interview, 3 May 1987.
10. Ibid.
11. Zindel, interview, 14 September 1984.
12. Zindel, interview, 10 May 1987.
13. Zindel, interview, 14 September 1984.
14. *Current Biography,* p. 445.
15. Zindel, interview, 10 May 1987.
16. *Current Biography,* p. 445.
17. Ruth Strickland, "Paul Zindel," in *Dictionary of Literary Biography: Twentieth Century American Dramatists, Part 2,* ed. John MacNicholas (Detroit, 1981), p. 369.
18. Zindel, interview, 10 May 1987.
19. Ibid.
20. Zindel, interview, 3 May 1987.
21. Zindel, interview, 19 May 1987.
22. Ibid.
23. Zindel, interview, 3 May 1987.
24. Ibid.
25. Ibid.
26. Ibid.

27. Zindel, interview, 10 May 1987.

28. Charlotte Zolotow, interview, 30 January 1987.

29. Anne Commire, ed., *Something about the Author* (Detroit, 1979), 16:283.

30. Zindel, interview, 26 May 1987, and Zolotow, interview, 30 January 1987.

31. Zindel, interview, 10 May 1987.

32. Ibid.

33. Zindel, interview, 3 May 1987.

34. Zindel, interview, 10 May 1987.

35. Zindel, interview, September 1984.

36. Zindel, interview, 10 May 1987.

37. Zindel, interview, 26 May 1987.

Chapter 2

1. Eaglen, "Of Life, Love," p. 180.

2. Zindel, interview, September 1984.

3. Paul Zindel, speech, Los Angeles Public Library, 20 May 1982.

4. Zindel, interview, 17 May 1987.

5. Aidan Chambers, "An Interview with Paul Zindel," *Times Literary Supplement,* September 1973, p. 229.

6. *Random House Dictionary of the English Language,* p. 681.

7. Chambers, "An Interview," p. 229.

8. Zindel, interview, 17 May 1987.

9. Eaglen, "Of Life, Love," p. 184.

10. Zindel, interview, 10 May 1987.

11. Zindel, interview, September 1984.

12. Eaglen, "Of Life, Love," pp. 181–82.

13. Kenneth Donelson and Alleen Pace Nilsen, *Literature for Today's Young Adults* (Glenview, Ill., 1980), p. 185.

14. *The Pigman* (New York, 1968); page numbers hereafter cited in the text.

15. Zindel, interview, 10 May 1987.

16. Ibid.

17. Ruth Robinson, review of *The Pigman, School Library Journal,* 15 November 1968, p. 4425.

18. Diane Farrell, review of *The Pigman, Horn Book,* February 1969, p. 61.

19. John Weston, review of *The Pigman, New York Times Book Review,* 3 November 1968, pt. 2, p. 2.

20. Lavinia Russ, review of *My Darling, My Hamburger, Publishers Weekly,* 22 September 1969.

21. *My Darling, My Hamburger* (New York, 1969); page numbers hereafter cited in the text.

22. Zindel, interview, 17 May 1987.

23. Diane Farrell, review of *My Darling, My Hamburger, Horn Book,* April 1970, p. 171.

24. Review of *My Darling, My Hamburger, Bulletin of the Center for Children's Books,* September 1970, p. 20.

25. Marilyn Singer, review of *My Darling, My Hamburger, Library Journal,* November 1969, p. 4303.

26. Zindel, interview, 17 May 1987.

27. *I Never Loved Your Mind* (New York, 1970); page numbers hereafter cited in the text.

28. Zindel, interview, 3 May 1987.

29. Diane Stavn, review of *I Never Loved Your Mind, Library Journal,* 15 June 1970, p. 2317.

30. Review of *I Never Loved Your Mind, Publishers Weekly,* 13 April 1970, p. 85.

31. Josh Greenfield, review of *I Never Loved Your Mind, New York Times Book Review,* 24 May 1970, pt. 2, p. 14.

32. Zindel, interview, 17 May 1987.

33. Ibid.

34. *Pardon Me, You're Stepping on My Eyeball* (New York, 1976); page numbers hereafter cited in the text.

35. Zindel, interview, 17 May 1987.

36. Ibid.

37. Review of *Pardon Me, Publishers Weekly,* 9 August 1976, p. 78.

38. Alix Nelson, review of *Pardon Me, New York Times Book Review,* 14 November 1976, p. 29.

39. Joan S. Brewer, review of *Pardon Me, School Library Journal,* October 1976, p. 121.

40. Review of *Pardon Me, Booklist,* 1 October 1976, p. 246.

41. Shirley Wilton, review of *Confessions, School Library Journal,* November 1977, p. 78.

42. Review of *Confessions, Publishers Weekly,* 19 September 1977, p. 146.

43. Zindel, interview, September 1984.

44. *Confessions of a Teenage Baboon* (New York, 1977); page numbers hereafter cited in the text.

45. Zindel, interview, 17 May 1987.

46. *The Undertaker's Gone Bananas* (New York, 1978); page numbers hereafter cited in the text.

47. Joyce Milton, review of *Undertaker, New York Times Book Review,* 10 December 1978, p. 88.

48. Karen Klockner, review of *Undertaker, Horn Book,* February 1979, p. 73.

49. Review of *Undertaker, Booklist,* 1 September 1978, p. 42.

50. Zindel, interview, 17 May 1987.

51. *The Pigman's Legacy* (New York, 1980); page numbers hereafter cited in the text.

52. Sally Holmes Holtze, review of *The Pigman's Legacy, School Library Journal,* October 1980, p. 160.

53. Paxton Davis, review of *The Pigman's Legacy, New York Times Book Review,* 25 January 1981, p. 27.

54. Review of *The Pigman's Legacy, Booklist,* 1 September 1980, p. 41.

55. *The Girl Who Wanted a Boy* (New York, 1981); page numbers hereafter cited in the text.

56. Zindel, interview, 19 May 1987.

57. Ibid.

58. Jean Mercier, review of *Girl Who Wanted a Boy, Publishers Weekly,* 6 November 1981, p. 79.

59. Stephanie Zvirin, review of *Girl Who Wanted a Boy, Booklist,* 1 September 1981, p. 38.

60. Robert Unsworth, review of *Girl Who Wanted a Boy, School Library Journal,* September 1981, p. 143.

61. Jean Fritz, review of *Girl Who Wanted a Boy, New York Times Book Review,* 15 November 1981, p. 58.

62. *Harry and Hortense at Hormone High* (New York, 1984); page numbers hereafter cited in the text.

63. Zindel, interview, September 1984 and 19 May 1987.

64. Patricia Campbell, review of *Harry and Hortense, Wilson Library Bulletin,* January 1985, p. 340.

65. Cathryn A. Male, review of *Harry and Hortense, School Library Journal,* October 1984, p. 172.

66. Charlotte Draper, review of *Harry and Hortense, Horn Book,* November 1984, p. 767.

67. Eaglen, "Of Life, Love," p. 184.

Chapter 3

1. Bonnie Zindel and Paul Zindel, *A Star for the Latecomer* (New York, 1980); page numbers hereafter cited in the text.

2. Jack Forman, review of *A Star for the Latecomer, School Library Journal,* April 1980, p. 129.

3. Review of *A Star for the Latecomer, Booklist,* 1 March 1980, p. 1045.

4. Zolotow, interview, January 1987, and Zindel, interview, 3 May 1987.

5. Crescent Dragonwagon, "Under a Good Star: Working with Paul Zindel," *ALAN Review,* Spring 1982, pp. 1–3.

6. Zindel, interview, 3 May 1987.

7. Ibid.

8. Dragonwagon, "Under a Good Star," pp. 2–3.

9. Ibid.

10. Crescent Dragonwagon and Paul Zindel, *To Take a Dare* (New York, 1982); page numbers hereafter cited in the text.

11. Dragonwagon, "Under a Good Star," p. 3.

12. Karen Ritter, review of *To Take a Dare, School Library Journal,* May 1982, pp. 68–69.

13. Joyce Milton, review of *To Take a Dare, New York Times Book Review,* 25 April 1982, p. 49.

14. Betty Carter, review of *To Take a Dare, English Journal,* September 1982, p. 88.

15. Alleen Pace Nilsen, "Bottoms Up in YA Literature," *Top of the News,* Fall 1983, p. 63.

16. *New York Times,* 19 May 1981, sec. 2, p. 6.

17. *School Library Journal,* August 1983, p. 2.

18. Ibid.

19. *I Love My Mother,* illus. John Melo (New York, 1975); page numbers hereafter cited in the text.

20. Marjorie Lewis, review of *I Love My Mother, School Library Journal,* April 1976, p. 68.

21. Review of *I Love My Mother, Bulletin of the Center for Children's Books,* January 1976, p. 88.

22. Zindel, interview, 3 May 1987.

23. *When a Darkness Falls* (New York, 1984); page numbers hereafter cited in the text.

24. Ann Fisher, review of *When a Darkness Falls, Library Journal,* 15 March 1985, p. 519.

25. Zindel, interview, 19 May 1987.

Chapter 4

1. Eaglen, "Of Life, Love," p. 180.

2. Zindel, interview, September 1984.

3. Zindel, interview, 19 May 1987.

4. Clive Barnes, review of *Gamma Rays, New York Times,* 8 April 1970, pt. 1, p. 32.

5. *The Effect of Gamma Rays on Man-in-the-Moon Marigolds* (New York, 1971); page numbers hereafter cited in the text.

6. Zindel, interview, 19 May 1987.

7. "Prizewinning Marigolds," *Time,* 17 May 1971, p. 66.

8. Ibid.

9. Zindel, interview, 26 May 1987.

10. *The Ladies Should Be in Bed* (New York, 1973); page numbers hereafter cited in the text.

11. Zindel, interview, 26 May 1987.

12. Ibid.

13. *Let Me Hear You Whisper* (New York, 1974); page numbers hereafter cited in the text.

14. Zindel, interview, 19 May 1987.

15. *And Miss Reardon Drinks a Little* (New York, 1971); page numbers hereafter cited in the text.

16. *The Secret Affairs of Mildred Wild* (New York, 1973); page numbers hereafter cited in the text.

17. *Ladies at the Alamo* (New York, 1977), p. 6; page numbers hereafter cited in the text.

18. Strickland, "Paul Zindel," p. 371.

19. Zindel, interview, 19 May 1987.

20. Paul Janeczko, "In Their Own Words: An Interview with Paul Zindel," *English Journal,* October 1977, pp. 20–21.

Chapter 5

1. Paul Janeczko, "Paul Zindel," in *From Writers to Students: The Pleasures and Pains of Writing,* ed. M. Jerry Weiss (Newark, Del., 1979), p. 111.

2. Zindel, interview, 10 May 1987.

3. Zolotow, interview, January 1987.

4. Janeczko, "Paul Zindel," p. 109.

5. Zindel, interview, 26 May 1987.

6. Ibid.

7. Zindel, interview, 3 May 1987.

8. Zindel, interview, 19 May 1987.

9. Ibid.

10. Zindel, interview, 10 May 1987.

11. Ibid.

12. Zindel, interview, 3 May 1987.

13. Zindel, interview, 10 May 1987.

14. Ibid.

Chapter 6

1. C. J. Thoman, Review of *Pardon Me, Best Sellers,* March 1977, p. 389.
2. Lillian Gerhardt, "Finn Pinn Award," *School Library Journal,* 15 April 1976, p. 45.
3. Eaglen, "Of Life, Love," p. 182.
4. Zindel, "The Magic of Special People," p. 31.
5. *The Ethics of the Fathers,* 1:14.
6. Eaglen, "Of Life, Love," p. 182.
7. Ibid., p. 179.
8. Ibid., p. 182.

Chapter 7

1. Eaglen, "Of Life, Love," p. 181.
2. Ibid.
3. Beverly Haley and Kenneth Donelson, "Pigs and Hamburgers, Cadavers and Gamma Rays: Paul Zindel's Adolescents," *Elementary English,* October 1974, p. 943.
4. James T. Henke, "Six Characters in Search of the Family: The Novels of Paul Zindel," in *Children's Literature* (Philadelphia, 1976), 5:131.
5. Zindel, interview, 10 May 1987.

Chapter 8

1. Eaglen, "Of Life, Love," p. 184.
2. Henke, "Six Characters," p. 135.

Chapter 9

1. Chambers, "An Interview," p. 243.

Chapter 10

1. Eaglen, "Of Life, Love," p. 181.
2. Review of *My Darling, My Hamburger, Publishers Weekly,* 22 September 1969, p. 95.

3. Chambers, "An Interview," p. 241.
4. Ibid., pp. 230–31.
5. Ibid., p. 239.
6. Ibid., p. 232.
7. Ibid.
8. Ibid.
9. Ibid., p. 233.
10. Henke, "Six Characters," p. 137.
11. Edward Albee, *The Zoo Story* (New York, 1960), p. 135.
12. Eaglen, "Of Life, Love," p. 183.
13. Zindel, interview, September 1984.

Chapter 11

1. All discussion in this section is based on an interview with Zindel on 26 May 1987.

Selected Bibliography

PRIMARY SOURCES

1. Young Adult Novels

The Amazing and Death-Defying Diary of Eugene Dingman. New York: Harper & Row, 1987.

Confessions of a Teenage Baboon. New York: Harper & Row, 1977; Bantam, 1978.

The Girl Who Wanted a Boy. New York: Harper & Row, 1981; Bantam, 1982.

Harry and Hortense at Hormone High. New York: Harper & Row, 1984; Harcourt Brace Jovanovich, 1984; Bantam, 1985.

I Never Loved Your Mind. New York: Harper & Row, 1970; Bantam, 1972.

My Darling, My Hamburger. New York: Harper & Row, 1969; Bantam, 1971.

Pardon Me, You're Stepping on My Eyeball. New York: Harper & Row, 1976; Bantam, 1977.

The Pigman. New York: Harper & Row, 1968; Bantam, 1981.

The Pigman's Legacy. New York: Harper & Row, 1980; Bantam, 1981.

The Undertaker's Gone Bananas. New York: Harper & Row, 1978; Bantam, 1979.

2. Young Adult Novels (Coauthor)

A Star for the Latecomer (by Bonnie Zindel). New York: Harper & Row, 1980; Bantam, 1981.

To Take a Dare (by Crescent Dragonwagon). New York: Harper & Row, 1982; Bantam, 1984.

3. Adult Novel

When a Darkness Falls. New York: Bantam Books, 1984.

4. Juvenile Novel

I Love My Mother. Illustrated by John Melo. New York: Harper & Row, 1975.

5. Plays

And Miss Reardon Drinks a Little. New York: Dramatists Play Service, 1971.
The Effect of Gamma Rays on Man-in-the-Moon Marigolds. New York: Dramatists Play Service; Harper & Row, 1971.
Ladies at the Alamo. New York: Dramatists Play Service, 1977.
The Ladies Should Be in Bed. New York: Dramatists Play Service, 1973.
Let Me Hear You Whisper. New York: Harper & Row, 1974, 1970; Dramatists Play Service, 1970.
The Secret Affairs of Mildred Wild. New York: Dramatists Play Service, 1973.

6. Unpublished Plays

Dimensions of Peacocks, 1959.
Euthanasia and the Endless Hearts, 1960.
A Dream of Swallows, 1962.

7. Articles

"The Magic of Special People." *School Media Quarterly,* Fall 1979, pp. 29–32+.
"The Theater Is Born within Us." *New York Times,* 26 July 1970, p. 1+ (theater section).

8. Speeches

Los Angeles Public Library, 20 May 1982 (on tape).
"The Magic of Special People." *School Media Quarterly,* Fall 1979, pp. 29–32+.
"Words into Life." *School Bookshop News,* Autumn 1978, pp. 22–24.

9. Screenplays and Teleplays

Alice in Wonderland–Through the Looking Glass, 1985 (CBS)
Babes in Toyland, 1986 (NBC)
Mame, 1974 (Warner Brothers)
Maria's Lovers, 1984 (Cannon Films)
Mrs. Beneker, 1971 (unproduced)
Runaway Train, 1985 (Cannon Films)
Up the Sandbox, 1972 (First Artists Films)

SECONDARY SOURCES

1. Books and Parts of Books

Albee, Edward. *The Zoo Story.* New York: Coward, 1960.
Commire, Anne, ed. *Something about the Author.* Detroit: Gale, 1979, 16:283.
Donelson, Kenneth, and Alleen Pace Nilsen. *Literature for Today's Young Adults.* Glenview, Ill.: Scott, Foresman & Co., 1980.
Fox, Geoff. "Paul Zindel." In *Twentieth Century Children's Writers.* Edited by D. L. Kirkpatrick. New York: St. Martin's Press, 1978, pp. 1383–84.
Henke, James T. "Six Characters in Search of the Family: The Novels of Paul Zindel." In *Children's Literature.* Philadelphia: Temple University Press, 1976, 5:130–40.
Rees, David. *The Marble in the Water: Essays on Contemporary Writers of Fiction for Children and Young Adults.* Boston: Horn Book Press, 1980, pp. 25–35.
Strickland, Ruth. "Paul Zindel." In *Dictionary of Literary Biography: Twentieth Century American Dramatists, Part 2.* Edited by John MacNicholas. Detroit: Gale, 1981, pp. 368–73.

2. Articles

Current Biography. New York: Wilson, 1973, pp. 445–48.
Dragonwagon, Crescent. "Under a Good Star: Working with Paul Zindel." *ALAN Review,* Spring 1982, pp. 1–3.
Gerhardt, Lillian. "Finn Pinn Award." *School Library Journal,* April 1976, p. 45.
Haley, Beverly A., and Kenneth Donelson. "Pigs and Hamburgers, Ca-

davers and Gamma Rays: Paul Zindel's Adolescents." *Elementary English,* October 1974, pp. 941–45.

Hoffmann, Stanley. "Winning, Losing, but Above All Taking Risks: A Look at the Novels of Paul Zindel." *Lion and the Unicorn,* Fall 1978, pp. 78–88.

Mercier, Jean. "Paul Zindel." *Publishers Weekly,* 5 December 1977, pp. 6–7.

Miner, M. D. "Grotesque Drama in the 70s." *Kansas Quarterly* 12, no. 4 (1980): 99–109.

Nilsen, Alleen Pace. "Bottoms Up in YA Literature." *Top of the News,* Fall 1983, pp. 62–67.

"Notes on People: Pulitzer Prize Winner Sued by Alleged Ghostwriter." *New York Times,* 19 May 1981, sec. 2, p. 6.

"Prizewinning Marigolds." *Time,* 17 May 1971, p. 66.

Stanek, Lou Willet. "The Junior Novel: A Stylistic Study." *Elementary English,* October 1974, pp. 947–53.

3. Interviews

Chambers, Aidan. "An Interview with Paul Zindel." *Times Literary Supplement* (London), September 1973, pp. 55+.

Eaglen, Audrey. "Of Life, Love, Death, Kids, and Inhalation Therapy: An Interview with Paul Zindel." *Top of the News,* Winter 1978, pp. 178–85.

Forman, Jack. Interviews with Paul Zindel: 14 September 1984 (Los Angeles); 3 May 1987; 10 May 1987; 17 May 1987; 19 May 1987; 26 May 1987 (by telephone).

———. Interview with Charlotte Zolotow. 30 January 1987 (by telephone).

Janeczko, Paul. "In Their Own Words: An Interview with Paul Zindel." *English Journal,* October 1977, pp. 20–21.

———. "Paul Zindel." In *From Writers to Students: The Pleasures and Pains of Writing.* Edited by M. Jerry Weiss. Newark, Del.: International Reading Association, 1979, pp. 107–13.

Warner, Craig. "Paul Zindel: From Idea to Script." *Hollywood Scriptwriter,* February 1984, pp. 1–6.

4. Book Reviews (Selected)

A. Young Adult Novels

Confessions of a Teenage Baboon

Benestad, Janet F. *Best Sellers,* February 1978, p. 368.

Bulletin of the Center for Children's Books, May 1978, p. 151.

Kirkus Reviews, 15 September 1977, p. 996.
Publishers Weekly, 19 September 1977, p. 146.
Wilton, Shirley. *School Library Journal,* November 1977, p. 78.

The Girl Who Wanted a Boy

Booklist, 1 September 1981, p. 38.
Bulletin of the Center for Children's Books, September 1981, p. 20.
Fritz, Jean. *New York Times Book Review,* 15 November 1981, p. 58.
Mitchell, J. N. *Voice of Youth Advocates (VOYA),* October 1981, p. 40.
Publishers Weekly, 6 November 1981, p. 79.
Unsworth, Robert. *School Library Journal,* September 1981, p. 143.

Harry and Hortense at Hormone High

Booklist, 1 September 1984, p. 60.
Bulletin of the Center for Children's Books, December 1984, p. 76.
Campbell, Patricia. *Wilson Library Bulletin,* January 1985, p. 340.
Draper, Charlotte. *Horn Book,* November-December 1984, p. 767.
Keresey, Gayle. *Voice of Youth Advocates (VOYA),* February 1985, p. 334.
Male, Cathryn. *School Library Journal,* October 1984, p. 172.
Publishers Weekly, 31 August 1984, p. 436.

I Never Loved Your Mind

Conner, John W. *English Journal,* December 1970, p. 1305.
Greenfield, Josh. *New York Times Book Review,* 24 May 1970, pt. 2, p. 14.
Kirkus Reviews, 15 May 1970, p. 560.
New Yorker, 5 December 1970, pp. 218–19.
Publishers Weekly, 13 April 1970, p. 85.
Stavn, Diane. *Library Journal,* 15 June 1970, p. 2317.

My Darling, My Hamburger

Bulletin of the Center for Children's Books, September 1970, p. 20.
Farrell, Diane. *Horn Book,* April 1970, p. 171.
Publishers Weekly, 22 September 1969, p. 85.
Singer, Marilyn. *Library Journal,* November 1969, p. 4303.
Townsend, John Rowe. *New York Times Book Review,* 9 November 1969, pt. 2, p. 2.

Pardon Me, You're Stepping on My Eyeball

Booklist, 1 October 1976, pp. 246, 258.
Brewer, J. S. *School Library Journal,* October 1976, p. 121.
Heins, Paul. *Horn Book,* October 1976, p. 505.

Nelson, Alix. *New York Times Book Review,* 14 November 1976, p. 29.
Publishers Weekly, 9 August 1976, p. 78.
Thoman, C. J. *Best Sellers,* March 1977, p. 389.

The Pigman
Booklist, 1 January 1969, p. 493.
Farrell, Diane. *Horn Book,* February 1969, p. 61.
Publishers Weekly, 30 September 1968, p. 61.
Robinson, Ruth. *Library Journal,* 15 November 1968, p. 4425.
Sutherland, Zena. *Saturday Review,* 18 January 1969, p. 4.
Weston, John. *New York Times Book Review,* 3 November 1968, pt. 2, p. 2.

The Pigman's Legacy
Bloom, W. B. *Voice of Youth Advocates (VOYA),* December 1980, p. 35.
Booklist, 1 September 1980, p. 41.
Bulletin of the Center for Children's Books, October 1980, p. 44.
Davis, Paxton. *New York Times Book Review,* 25 January 1981, p. 27.
Heins, Paul. *Horn Book,* October 1980, p. 531.
Holtze, Sally Holmes. *School Library Journal,* October 1980, p. 160.
Seventeen, June 1982, p. 56.

The Undertaker's Gone Bananas
Booklist, 1 September 1978, p. 42.
Klockner, K. M. *Horn Book,* February 1979, p. 73.
Milton, Joyce. *New York Times Book Review,* 10 December 1978, p. 88.
Unsworth, Robert. *School Library Journal,* October 1978, p. 160.
Weinstein, Bernard. *Best Sellers,* March 1979, p. 411.

B. Young Adult Novels (Co-author)

A Star for the Latecomer
Booklist, 15 March 1980, p. 1045.
Bulletin of the Center for Children's Books, May 1980, p. 184.
Flowers, A. A. *Horn Book,* June 1980, p. 310.
Forman, Jack. *School Library Journal,* April 1980, p. 129.
Jaffee Cyrisse. *New York Times Book Review,* 20 July 1980, p. 17.
Schmitz, E. *Best Sellers,* May 1980, p. 80.

To Take a Dare
Bulletin of the Center for Children's Books, April 1982, p. 145.
Campbell, Patricia. *Wilson Library Bulletin,* February 1981, pp. 454–55.

Carter, Betty. *English Journal,* September 1982, p. 88.
Milton, Joyce. *New York Times Book Review,* 25 April 1982, p. 49.
Publishers Weekly, 19 March 1982, p. 71.
Ritter, Karen. *School Library Journal,* May 1982, p. 68.

C. Juvenile Book

I Love My Mother
America, 6 December 1975, p. 401.
Bulletin of the Center for Children's Books, January 1976, p. 88.
Lewis, Marjorie. *School Library Journal,* April 1976, p. 68.
Publishers Weekly, 20 October 1975, p. 71.

D. Plays

And Miss Reardon Drinks a Little
Nation, 15 March 1971, pp. 347–48.
New York, 15 March 1971, pp. 46+.
New Yorker, 6 March 1971, p. 67.
Playboy, June 1971, pp. 46+.
Saturday Review, 20 March 1971, p. 10.
Time, 8 March 1971, p. 47.

The Effect of Gamma Rays on Man-in-the-Moon Marigolds
Avant, John Alfred. *Library Journal,* 15 January 1971, p. 204.
Barnes, Clive. *New York Times,* 8 April 1970, sec. I, p. 32.
Booklist, 1 September 1971, p. 28.
Choice, December 1971, p. 1340.
Cosgrove, Mary. *Horn Book,* June 1971, p. 308.
Kirkus Reviews, 1 February 1971, p. 166; 15 February 1971, p. 185.
Life, 4 July 1970, pp. 8–9.
Newsweek, 27 April 1970, p. 64.
New Yorker, 18 April 1970, pp. 82+.
Saturday Review, 2 May 1970, p. 12.
Time, 20 April 1970, p. 51.

Ladies at the Alamo
New Yorker, 18 April 1977, p. 102.
New York Times, 8 April 1977, sec. III, p. 3; 17 April 1977, sec. II, p. 3.
Time, 18 April 1977, p. 31.

Let Me Hear You Whisper
Bulletin of the Center for Children's Books, July 1974, p. 188.
Choice, September 1974, p. 950.

English Journal, January 1975, p. 112; February 1975, p. 98.
Gerhardt, Lillian. *Library Journal,* 15 April 1974, p. 1234.
Publishers Weekly, 28 January 1974, p. 300.

The Secret Affairs of Mildred Wild

Nation, 4 December 1972, p. 573.
Newsweek, 27 November 1972, p. 77.
New Yorker, 25 November 1972, pp. 111–12.
New York Times, 15 November 1972, p. 38.
Time, 27 November 1972, p. 73.

Index of Characters

Characters are alphabetized by last name first.

Index of Subjects

score score

About the Author

Jack Jacob Forman is a librarian at Mesa Community College in San Diego. For the past two decades, he has held a variety of public service, consultative, and administrative positions in public and academic libraries. The author of several articles in publications such as *Horn Book, School Library Journal,* and the *San Diego Union, he has also published book reviews in Library Journal, School Library Journal, Top of the News,* and the *New York Times Book Review.* He and his wife, a teacher of English as a second language, have lived in San Diego for ten years.